Cra

Crash The Fed
©2025 Dan Taxation Is Theft Behrn

How does one who does not believe in the use of government force to protect intellectual property copyright their material? Simple. This copyright is not enforced by registration with the government. I claim the copyright because I am the creator.

By purchasing this book or accepting it as a gift or by any other means, you agree to the following terms:

You will not copy large portions of the book or as a whole without express authorization by the original author.

You can quote any original content in this book as long as you cite the book as a source.

If this is a printed copy of the book, you may lend it or sell it to any person, but only if you advise them that by receiving the book, they are in agreement with the terms herein.

Release Version: 1.0.2

They will not force us,
They will stop degrading us,
They will not control us,
And we will be victorious.
— Muse

To Ron Paul —

Whose unwavering voice
cracked the walls of the temple.

And to everyone who knows
freedom isn't given, it's taken.

Table of Contents

Preface: In Dialogue with Ron Paul..9

A Note on Terms..11

Introduction...15

Part I Understanding The Enemy...23
    Freedom, Force, and Violence...25
    Legal Tender and Constitutional Betrayal...33
    Whatever Goes Up Must Come Down...43
    The Fed's Perpetual Debt Machine..49

Part II The Illusion of Political Solutions...59
    Why Voting Won't Save Us...61
    The Left–Right Divide as a Distraction...65
    Lessons from History...69

Part III Crashing The Fed..75
    Understanding Markets...77
    The Real-World Consequences..85
    Preparing For the Crash..91
    What Happens to the Dollar...99
    Avoiding a Fed 2.0..103

Part IV Starving The Beast..111
    Disclaimer..113
    Withdrawing Consent..113
    Loot the Treasury..119
    Trading Paper for Value..129

Part V Packing The Parachute...137
    Building Parallel Systems..139
    Local Currencies...145
    Alternative Financial Networks...146

Part VI The End Game..151
    Signs of Imminent Collapse..153
    Controlled Demolition...159

Preface: In Dialogue with Ron Paul

In 2009, Ron Paul published *End the Fed*, a book that peeled back the curtain on one of the most destructive institutions in American history. He explained its origins, its secrecy, and its role in robbing generations of their wealth and liberty. He made the case — moral, constitutional, and economic — for ending it.

But more than a decade later, the Fed still stands. Its power has grown, not shrunk. And the politicians who promised to "audit" or "reform" it, have either failed, sold out, or been crushed by the system they hoped to change.

This book picks up where *End the Fed* left off. It is both a tribute to Ron Paul's clarity and a refusal to accept half-measures. Where *End The Fed* laid the philosophical foundation and exposed how the Fed works, *Crash the Fed* gives practical steps we can all take to end it once and for all. The Fed will not be voted away. If we are not vigilant, the system that props up the Fed will replace it with something even worse.

If you've read *End the Fed*, this book will feel like a continuation — one that sharpens the blade and aims it squarely at the root. If you haven't, you'll still find here everything you need to understand the problem, why politics won't solve it, and what we can do that will.

End the Fed is the why. *Crash the Fed* is the how.

A Note on Terms

There are a few terms that I will use throughout the book that you may already be familiar with. I'll go over them briefly in case you are not.

Bail-ins – When banks use depositors' money to stabilize themselves during a crisis instead of relying on outside bailouts. This means customer funds can be seized to cover bank losses.

Bailouts – When governments or central banks use taxpayer money or newly created money to rescue failing banks or corporations. Marketed as "saving the economy," but usually protecting elites from their own bad bets.

Blockchain – A technology that is a public ledger in which everyone can see all the transactions, but only the holder of a private key can authorize the transfer of a digital currency from one account to another. These chains are immutable, as each sequence of events has a verification of the events before. If the history of a single transaction were changed, everyone would know immediately. Millions of copies of the chain are saved on "nodes" around the world, some held by large organizations and millions held by individuals.

CBDC (Central Bank Digital Currency) – A government-issued digital form of money that allows authorities to directly monitor, restrict, or program how money is used. Marketed as modernization, but designed for total control. One proposed measure is money that expires if not spent.

Central Bank – An institution, like the Federal Reserve, that issues currency, controls interest rates, and manages a nation's monetary policy. Central banks serve governments and financial elites, not the public. Most other banks have a forced relationship with the central bank, turning the whole system into a cartel.

CPI (Consumer Price Index) – The government's official measure of inflation, based on a "basket" of goods. Often manipulated through substitutions or weighting to understate the true rise in the cost of living.

Debt Ceiling – The legal cap on how much debt the U.S. government can incur. It is routinely raised by Congress to allow more borrowing, making it more of a political show than a real limit.

Federal Reserve Note (FRN) – Federal Reserve Notes are private IOUs issued by the Federal Reserve Bank. They will be abbreviated as FRNs throughout this book. These are commonly referred to simply as "Dollars."

Fiat Currency – Paper or digital money declared legal by government decree but not backed by physical assets like gold or silver. Its value comes from forced acceptance, not intrinsic worth or public consensus.

Fractional Reserve Banking – A system where banks keep only a fraction of deposits as reserves while lending out the rest. This multiplies credit beyond actual savings and makes banks fragile in crises.

Hyperinflation – A collapse in confidence in a currency, where prices skyrocket so fast that money loses value daily or even hourly. Examples include Weimar Germany and Zimbabwe.

Inflation – The loss of a currency's purchasing power as more units are created. This is not a natural rise in prices, but the direct result of money printing or other manipulation.

Legal Tender – A law requiring citizens to accept government-issued money as payment for debts. This forces people to use fiat currency even when they would prefer alternatives.

Monetary Policy – The set of actions central banks take to control the money supply and interest rates. Often presented as science, but in reality it is manipulation that benefits the political and financial class.

Parallel Economy – A system of trade and finance that operates outside government-controlled money, such as barter, crypto, or local community currencies.

Stimulus – Government spending or handouts (commonly funded by new money creation) intended to "boost" the economy. In reality, it's a short-term sugar high that deepens long-term inflation. It's often given to the public to distract from bigger problems or even political fraud.

Introduction

Every great crime begins with a lie. The lie of the Federal Reserve is that it exists to stabilize the economy, protect your savings, and ensure prosperity for all. In reality, it's a wealth-extraction machine — a cartel of bankers and politicians who control the money supply for their own benefit, at your expense. It is used to silently steal your spending power and stick it right in their pockets. Most people never know this is happening because the money in their wallet and the numbers on their bank account stay the same. The value is quietly stolen, and moved to someone else's control in broad daylight.

If that sounds extreme, ask yourself three simple questions:
- Who controls the money?
- Who benefits when more of it is created?
- Who pays the price when its value collapses?

The answers aren't complicated, but they are deeply uncomfortable: the insiders at the top reap the gains, while everyone else foots the bill.

When I first learned how the system really works, I was furious. Not because it was wrong (which it is), but because it was *invisible* to most people. Worse than that, people are conditioned to reject truth, believing that the Federal Reserve is what keeps the economy stable. We are trained from childhood to believe that inflation is "natural," that debt is "normal," and that our only real choice is between left and right — two wings of the same predatory bird.

That conditioning began for me before I could even spell "economics." I remember my first collision with an economic rule I couldn't escape: sales tax. When I was younger, I was given a remote control car as a gift. Batteries not included. I scraped together everything I had and walked to the neighborhood grocery store. The price tag on a pack of batteries said $2.50, I only had $2.00, so I walked home and tore the house apart to find the extra fifty cents. I walked back to the store, picked up the batteries and went to the register to check out. I was embarrassed to learn I didn't have enough because the price was now $2.71. The rule was the rule: no payment, no batteries. At the time, I didn't know it, but that little "extra" was part of a much larger machine — one designed to take from me before I even understood the game.

Years later, as I built my first business, I came to understand the game in clearer terms. It wasn't just about taxes — it was about **control**. The people who control the money supply don't need to take from you directly. Instead of taking things where you would notice the numbers missing, they could steal the buying power of your hard-earned money from thousands of miles away. The money stays in your wallet or your bank account, but the value goes down as the value of their accounts go up by simply creating more.

They can dilute the value of every dollar in your pocket without asking your permission. They can decide when credit is cheap, when it's scarce, and when the whole economy will "mysteriously" slow down — and they'll do it in ways that keep you blaming the wrong people.

I've seen it up close. During my time in politics, I watched as entire communities were kept dependent on unstable currency, cheap credit, and government programs that inflated today's prosperity at the cost of tomorrow's struggle. When the Fed floods the system with easy money, it's like throwing a party with someone else's credit card — fun for a while, until the bill comes due. And when the crash hits, the people at the top already have their escape routes planned, while everyone else is left confused, scared and in serious trouble.

But there is another assumption that we all hold, even though we should reject it. We believe that when the government borrows money and goes into debt, we are putting future generations on the hook to repay that money. But that couldn't be further from the truth. When the government prints money, it goes into debt. That debt is never meant to be repaid. In fact, it's quite literally impossible. Through the relationship with the Federal Reserve, that debt creates an income stream for a private bank. The interest on that debt creates more debt than there is money.

We are not on the hook for this. None of us signed for, approved, accepted, or received any of that debt. It's a contract that is not in our name. Just like any corporation that protects its officers, investors, and employees from ever having to pay back corporate debt, the public is not on the hook for the government's debt.

When I ran for president in 2020, I made the Federal Reserve my central target. At campaign events, I'd ask people simple questions:
- "If your boss cut your paycheck by 15%, would you notice?"
- "If prices at the grocery store doubled in two years, would you feel robbed?"
- "What if I told you both of those things are happening — just through different levers?"

To drive this point home and showcase the ridiculousness of the Fed, I printed my own money. This wasn't anything illegal. It wasn't counterfeiting, and it wasn't completely worthless. I created an IOU, just like the Federal Reserve. Believe it or not, that's real money – a real security that can be reported to the FEC. Because if my campaign ever came to me and demanded that I fulfill my end of the obligation, I would be required to give $50 million of my own personal money to the campaign. The campaign could use this IOU like any other security.

Could I have paid the $50 million if they demanded it? No, but luckily I was in charge of the campaign and knew that would never happen. Could I have taken it to a bank and deposited it? Not likely. If I did, they'd come back to me personally, demanding the $50 million which I wouldn't be able to pay and would have to declare bankruptcy. At that point I might even be charged with fraud. But I never let that happen.

So isn't it completely worthless? Not completely. First, it was an excellent demonstration of how the government creates money. This helped a lot of people understand that the Federal Reserve and their notes were a complete scam.

Second, it got me into a few debates, where eligibility was determined by the amount of money that the candidates had raised. I didn't have the resources that some of the other candidates had, so this helped me cross those lines. It also got me into the top 10 list of presidential candidates on the 2020 FEC report. I out-raised Kamala Harris and Andrew Yang, two of those most popular primary candidates in 2020 that are still politically active today.

It didn't matter if I was in a union hall, a libertarian meetup, or a college auditorium — the moment I explained that inflation is not some act of God, but a policy choice made by people with names, addresses, and political allies, the room changed. People realized this wasn't abstract economics. This was **theft through the control of money itself, and slavery through the vacuum of debt.**

Once you see it, you can't unsee it:
- The Fed decides how easy or hard it is for you to buy a home.
- The Fed decides whether your retirement account is going to support you when you stop getting paychecks.
- The Fed decides if your wages keep up with your bills or quietly fall behind.

And yet, most people don't even know the names of the people making those calls. That's not an accident — it's by design.

Many others have already attempted to rip the mask off that design. I don't feel that I need to do what's already been done. And if you've picked up this book, you likely already know what the Federal Reserve is all about.

Instead, I'll show you how to start insulating yourself, your family, and your community from the fallout, and how to proactively work towards ending the Fed. The end is inevitable, but most of us are not as prepared as we should be. If we can stop them from kicking the can down the road, we'll spend less time suffering. The bandage needs to be ripped off.

I didn't set out to be a political figure or activist. I set out to be free — free from control by tyrants who want to control me and my productivity, and take what I have without my consent. I've fought their machines – from their parking enforcers to the IRS and the FEC. I learned how they operate. I learned how they respond. And I've got a pretty solid record of winning. All it takes is a solid understanding of how they lie.

Control the money, control the people. That's the real story of the Federal Reserve. And if we don't challenge that control, every other political fight is just theater.

No one is coming to save us. We have to save ourselves. This book will show you how.

What Is This Book?

If you've ever had a deep conversation with someone about government, politics, economics, or philosophy, you've likely encountered the "pills." This metaphor originated from The Matrix, where Neo, played by Keanu Reeves, was asked to take a red pill or a blue pill. The red pill would wake him up to see the world as it truly was, and the blue pill would make him forget everything and live his life in ignorant bliss.

Since then, many have taken this metaphor and adapted it to various other contexts. The red pill is still often used in the same way politically, where someone who is "red-pilled" is said to understand the way the world really works. Their eyes are open. They know secrets that most people never care to acknowledge. Some of them are in plain view, ignored by those who refuse to open their eyes.

This collection of pills has also been expanded to include other colors. Those who are "orange-pilled" are into crypto, the color orange coming from the Bitcoin logo.

Then there are black and white pills. The "black-pilled" are the people who believe that everything is a disaster, heading to absolute chaos and destruction. They believe the government, the money, society, and everything else is going to collapse. They anticipate World War III at any moment. Though they are often not panicked, they have just accepted that this is the way things are.

The white-pilled on the other hand, recognize that society faces the same problems as the black pilled, but they believe that humanity is stronger than its problems. The white pilled believe that, though we may be struggling now, there is a light at the end of the tunnel. They believe we can overcome human suffering, war, economic problems, crime, and everything else.

While this book advocates for ending the Fed, I may sound like I am black-pilled. But don't be mistaken, I am very white-pilled. I do believe that the Fed is a massive problem creating struggle, not just for every American, but for many people throughout the world. My optimism is that it can and will be defeated.

Many people assume that I am a Libertarian, as that is where you will find the most fervent Ron Paul fanatics. Though the libertarian philosophy often attracts a mix of limited government minarchists and anarchists, the official Libertarian party inherently believes that the way to fix things is through the political system. There is a smaller group that overlaps with libertarians, and they are referred to as "collapsi-tarians." You might find after reading this book that this philosophy more accurately describes me. You won't find a definition in a dictionary because many people will debate the particulars of what makes one a collapsitarian. However, after reading this book, you might believe that this term accurately describes me.

I don't have much faith in voting for major change. Instead, I believe the only way to eliminate socially destructive systems is to just stand back and let them collapse under their own weight. If anything, I might give it a little push. I find it a waste of energy to try to fix systems that are destined for failure. It only results in those systems needlessly sticking around and harming millions of people for decades or centuries.

With the Fed, people often want to slow the printing machine, then eliminate it, then replace it with sound money. What I hope to convince you is that slowing the printing will only make the Fed appear stable, prolonging its existence. Accelerating the printing will make more people realize the Fed is the problem and must be eliminated. When they realize this, they won't wait around for politicians to do something–they will stop using dollars and use better currencies. The Fed will still exist, but it will be completely removed from everyone's lives by their own intent.

Who Am I?

Of course, you are wondering who I am and why I would have any solutions that you haven't heard before.

At the time of this writing, I haven't had a driver's license in nearly twenty years. I have driven my car unregistered for much of that time. I have received several parking and traffic tickets, many citing driving without a license or driving without registration. I haven't paid a single one. Most are completely removed from the system before I even have a chance to fight them.

I haven't paid income tax in about ten years. For a few years that I had money withheld from my employer, I was given a full refund from the IRS. Not just the income tax, but Social Security, Medicare and every other payment that was made to them.

I don't advocate borrowing with the intent of not repaying, but when I was young I found myself buried in debt. I was working for a company that was falling apart and couldn't pay what they owed me. I tried working with creditors, only to find out how they operated like criminals. I tried debt consolidation and other main-stream approaches to get myself out from under this. But most of these systems seemed to be just another predatory end of the same banks. I found myself on payment plans where the balance would continue to increase each month.

When I had enough, I just stopped paying. I looked into the legal system, learned a few laws, and how banks actually work. I stopped paying. I beat credit cards with balances of $10,000 or more by refusing to pay. I was sued by one, but they withdrew their case after I demanded to see proof that I owed them anything. A close friend was sued for a similar reason, and I wrote his response. His case was withdrawn as well.

What about my credit? I was able to erase most of this debt off of my credit report fairly quickly. One was a lien from the IRS. I mentioned I haven't paid taxes in about ten years. Ten years before that I tried the same, but didn't have enough knowledge to accomplish what I do now. Instead, I learned that the IRS has an account status called Currently Not Collectable (CNC). I got myself on this list, and the IRS never tried to collect a penny from me, until the debt expired. But this did come with a mark on my credit. Out of curiosity, I challenged that mark the same way I challenged the credit cards, and it was promptly removed.

Aside from my political and bureaucratic shenanigans, I am an engineer. I have worked for several mega corporations over the past two decades, where I was responsible for overseeing systems that conducted billions of dollars in transactions. In some cases, there were billions of transactions that were only a few cents, but added up to large amounts.

Knowing how these systems work isn't enough. It is crucial to know every path a packet of data can follow through, the consequences of each stop, the importance of ordering, and any potential for a packet to be lost and forgotten. Small software bugs can cause these companies to lose millions of dollars in a day.

Finding these flaws and fixing them isn't always difficult. Sometimes once the problem is identified, the source of the problem is another company or even another team within the company. We can beg and plead with those companies or teams to fix their issue, but it might not be as important to them as it is to my team. We can fly it up the flag pole and try to get executives to pressure those other companies or teams, but often they don't care about these problems or have bigger issues to deal with.

Even though these problems are out of our control, it is our responsibility to fix them. And we do. Because the problems are caused by systems that are out of our control, we have to get creative. We have to understand that we can sit around pointing the blame at others, or we can take action ourselves.

This isn't just software. I take the same approach when dealing with scammers, from banks to bureaucrats. When financial institutions try to rob me, I know that trying to navigate through customer service lines is futile. There are so many ways to leverage the same legal system that they abuse, to beat them at their own games. I won't get into the details of those methods too much in this book, but it is analogous to ending the Fed.

Calling our representatives is futile. Protesting is futile. Talking about it on talk shows and podcasts is futile. The problem exists in a system over which we have no control. The people running that system know it's a problem for us, but it's not a problem for them. They aren't going to fix it. It is our job to find creative solutions to end the Fed without them. This is my skill set.

Part I
Understanding The Enemy

You never give me your money,
You only give me your funny paper,
And in the middle of negotiations,
You break down.
— The Beatles

Part I
Understanding the Enquiry

Freedom, Force, and Violence

The air inside the convention hall was thick with noise. *"End the Fed! End the Fed!"* chants rippled through the crowd—echoing off high ceilings until it felt like the room itself was vibrating. This wasn't a campaign stop for a polished politician or a corporate economic summit. It was Ron Paul standing behind a simple wooden podium, sleeves rolled up, looking more like a small-town doctor than a revolutionary.

But a revolutionary is exactly what he was.

I remember watching from the side of the stage as he declared, "We don't need to just *audit* the Federal Reserve—we need to abolish it." The crowd erupted—not because they'd dissected *The Creature from Jekyll Island,* but because they *felt* the truth in their bones. They knew something was deeply wrong. They were waiting for someone to call it out.

Yet when the "Audit the Fed" bill reached Congress, even supposed allies abandoned it. Bernie Sanders, once a backer, gutted it in committee, stripping away the transparency it aimed to bring. The establishment, left and right, closed ranks.

That's when it became clear: You don't beat a rigged game by asking the dealer for a better hand.

True freedom is the power to resist control.

The prescription isn't more elections or transparency—it's leveraging force: coordinated, non-violent resistance that makes systems unworkable without our compliance.

Think Montgomery Bus Boycotts in 1955. It didn't reform segregation through appeals—it economically strangled its opponents. That is the model for confronting the Fed: make the system unprofitable to operate.

The Myth of the Gentle Path

We've been conditioned to believe that if we just vote harder, if we elect the "right" people, the system will fix itself. Be civilized. History tells a different story.

Martin Luther King Jr. didn't win his rights by waiting politely for better cabinet appointments. He didn't appeal for gentler oppression. He forced change through organized boycott, marching, and deliberate defiance of unjust laws. He used **force**, not violence, force as the strength of organized, peaceful resistance against the violence of an unjust system.

This distinction matters. **Force** is the capacity to act, to resist, to stand firm, to push back, and to defend. **Violence** is a violation of rights, life, or property, accomplished through physical force, fraud, or coercion.

A mugger with a knife is plainly violent. A banker debasing your wages by printing money is economic violence—no blood spilled, but your right to spending power violated.

Smart governments often pride themselves on free speech and the right to protest, as long as it's done peacefully. While this is sometimes a useful tool, it is often used to pacify us. By letting the steam out of the kettle, we are less likely to forcefully rebel against the government. While these rights appear to work out in our favor, they often work out in the government's favor.

Think about the American Revolution. It started out with demands and protests. Those demands and protests were met with force and violence by the British authorities. It continued to escalate until the revolution became violent.

Imagine what would have happened if the British had never used force. Imagine if instead, the red coats kept taking the colonists' demands back to the king. The king would continuously relay back that he would love to help them, but he can't for one excuse or another. He would tell them now is not the time. He would cite experts that say the colony's demands for lower taxes and more freedom would ultimately destroy the economy. He might even point blame at some other country.

As long as the king never incited violence against the people, they could exercise their free speech all day. The king might actively miseducate most of the population into believing that high taxes and little freedom were good for them. This would keep the rebels to a minimum, and their own countrymen would turn against them.

Then, when the rebels had enough and started using force against British soldiers, they would be the ones who look like the violent loonies. "Why would you act so violently against our benevolent king? Look at everything he has done for us!"

Those rights could have radically altered the course of history if we had them in the past, and if they were used to successfully pacify the revolution. Today we are faced with a question – are we settling for abuse because our right to talk about it is preventing us from acting?

The Fed's Violence Wears a Suit

When the Federal Reserve expands the money supply, it's not a neutral policy tweak — it's the erosion of your wealth. You earn, you save — then the Fed unilaterally says your money now buys less.

This is inflation: the hidden tax. Unlike the mugger, the Fed does it with acronyms and media narratives — QE, ZIRP, CPI, Bailouts, Stimulus — framed as saving the economy, when it's really destroying it.

Ron Paul was right when he said the Fed enables ceaseless war, bailouts, and government overreach. Stripped of its unlimited printing press, the government would have to face the public directly: raise taxes or cut spending. Printing money circumvents consent.

What Does Ending the Fed Mean?

Some people interpret "ending the Fed" as a return to a gold standard. For centuries, gold and silver had been the standard money used by governments around the world. They would issue their own currency which would be redeemable in these metals. If buyers from one country wanted to buy goods from another country, they could trade different currencies on an international exchange. But when the trade imbalance got too big, a country could buy back their notes with gold, instead of letting the other country dump their currency on the exchange, lowering its value.

When it comes to ending the Fed, we have to understand that changing legal tender laws or adding a gold backing to the currency aren't viable solutions on their own.

In an interview with Peter Robinson, Thomas Sowell was asked why he supports Ron Paul's position on ending the Fed, and if the Fed were removed, what would it be replaced with? Sowell brilliantly replied, "When someone removes a cancer what do you replace it with?"

This is great in theory, but it misses a harsh reality. If you end the Fed, all the money we have today becomes worthless. Is our entire society meant to operate without money from that point forward?

If the question of replacing the Fed is whether it would be replaced with some other central banking scheme, then of course it should be replaced with nothing.

But what will replace the money that we use today? And how will that transition occur? It's a great fantasy to believe we can just press the Rothbard button and make the Fed go away. But in the real world, there will be consequences. We might not need a central authority to make that decision for us, but we should understand what needs to happen and start planning for what's coming.

Changing legal tender laws to only allow gold or silver would still mean that we accept the government's authority to alter contracts and force them to be payable in whatever they decide. Gold today, back to paper tomorrow. Issuing a new gold backed currency only takes us back 50 years into the same position we were in before – a government controlled currency that can easily be taken back off the gold standard whenever the government has an emergency.

This is all irrelevant, as trying to back the current currency with gold is impossible. The government doesn't have enough gold to back the notes in circulation. If they tried to buy gold by printing the money, the inflation they caused would keep pricing themselves out of the market. When people know the government is buying gold because the dollar is becoming worthless, they will not sell. Nobody will sell gold to the government for notes that will be backed by a smaller amount of gold.

The Debt Spiral

Central banking guarantees endless debt. Picture this: the Fed lends the government $100 at 1% interest. A year later, the government owes $101, but only $100 exists. So it must borrow more, just to pay the interest. That's by design, not by accident.

As former Fed Chairman Alan Greenspan famously said on *Meet the Press*: "The United States can pay any debt it has because we can always print money to do that. So there is zero probability of default." More recently, Neel Kashkari, president of the Fed of Minneapolis, said on *60 Minutes*, "Your banks are safe, there's enough cash in the financial system and there is an infinite amount of cash at the Federal Reserve." This has been repeated by other Fed chairmen throughout the years, and it makes one thing clear. There will not be another bank run, as they will all be suppressed with an infinite supply of printed money.

That's not fiscal vigor. It's the banking cartel intentionally trapping the government in perpetual debt. It's mathematically impossible to pay such a debt. The money itself *is* debt. They must continue to borrow just to keep the lights on.

Why would the banks lend money to someone that they know they can't repay? Because they can force them to make payments, and those payments will result in a net positive, more than they ever could have bought with their original investment.

Let's look at a short version of the Fed's history. We all know the Federal Reserve was created in 1913, initially raising about $100 million by selling stock to member banks. It could be said that the bank now had this $100 million available on deposit to lend back to banks as the "lender of last resort." There weren't any Federal Reserve Notes until 1914, when the government started printing them at the Bureau of Engraving and Printing, not at the Federal Reserve. The government didn't borrow any money from the Fed until 1917, when they borrowed a small $50 million to fund the first World War.

In 1913, the GDP was about $40 billion. That $100 million valuation meant this bank could have purchased about 2.5 tenths of a percent of everything the county produced. While that's still a lot, it's relatively little.

In 2024 the GDP grew to nearly $30 trillion. But the Federal Reserve's assets are now valued at about $6 trillion. Mostly making their money through interest that can not be escaped, the bank's assets have grown to about 20% of the GDP. Adjusting for inflation, that's a 10,000% growth, and as long as they continue to charge interest, it will continue to grow. Yet they have produced and contributed nothing of real value to the economy.

This trap is absolutely intentional. While some people view it as a biblical crime for banks to charge interest at all, most bank loans can be paid off. If the borrower can't afford it, they can declare bankruptcy, and the bank loses for making a bad investment. But when the issuer of money can charge interest at the source, the debt becomes absolutely impossible to pay off. While congress is able to declare bankruptcy and nullify this debt, they don't seem interested at all. They enjoy too many benefits from this system to ever terminate it. The bank knows this, and does what it can to keep Congress happy and protect their very existence.

Of course, increased GDP is always touted as proof that the economy is doing well, and never as a sign of inflation. But the real question is how much value was produced. Imagine the entire economy consists of 100 factories with a GDP of $1 million. If the Fed prints a bunch of money, the GDP will rise to $100 million in ten years. Even if the output of those factories remained exactly the same, with zero growth, economists would cheer on the growing GDP. It's a misdirection to cover the debt. Sure, the debt might be at an all-time high of $40 trillion, but it's still only a small amount higher than the GDP. Comparing the debt to the GDP doesn't really tell you much at all. If anything it tells you how much money is sitting idle versus how much is being spent – and that tells you very little about how productive the economy is.

There's a joke about two economists walking together. One notices a pile of dog shit and says to the other, "I'll pay you $100 to eat that pile of shit." The second economist takes the $100 and eats the pile of shit.

They continue walking until the second economist sees another pile of shit and says "I'll pay you $100 to eat that pile of shit." The first economist takes the $100 and eats a pile of shit.

Walking a little more, the first economist looks at the second and says, "You know, I gave you $100 to eat shit, then you gave me back the same $100 to eat shit. I can't help but feel like we both just ate shit for nothing."

"That's not true", responded the second economist. "We increased the GDP by $200!"

The Road Ahead

Ron Paul's crowds proved something: people will rally to a cause they barely understand if they intuit its existential threat. The challenge is turning that intuition into clear understanding, and then into collective action.

This isn't about waiting for Congress. It's about finding a strategy that we the people can employ, and taking direct action to shut down the Fed.

Force is our capacity to act. **Violence** is what we endure when we don't. The question isn't if the Fed will fall—it's when and how. Sooner is better than later, and a controlled demolition that favors the people over a corrupt banking cartel is favorable.

Legal Tender and Constitutional Betrayal

The United States Constitution says that no state shall "make any Thing but gold and silver Coin a Tender in Payment of Debts." Many people read that and conclude that the federal government violated the Constitution by declaring Federal Reserve Notes to be legal tender. There is plenty of debate here.

The restriction in Article I, Section 10 is aimed at the states. The federal government is not expressly mentioned there. That gap set the stage for a long legal and political struggle over who, if anyone, may force paper on the public.

That brings us to the Tenth Amendment and the basic structure of federal power. The Constitution grants Congress enumerated powers: to tax, to borrow, to coin money and regulate its value, to fix standards of weights and measures, and so on. It does not grant a power to declare paper notes legal tender. Meanwhile, the states are explicitly barred from making anything but gold and silver coins a legal tender. What follows from that pairing is simple: if Congress was not given a power, and the states are forbidden from it, then no government possesses it. The Tenth Amendment says the powers not delegated to the United States are reserved to the states or to the people. Since the states can't exercise a legal-tender-paper power, and Congress wasn't granted it, the power belongs to no one. The federal government's claim to it is usurpation, plain and simple.

By the time of the Civil War, Congress had already taken the plunge. It passed the Legal Tender Acts of 1862–63, authorizing so-called "Greenbacks" and declaring those paper notes "lawful money and a legal tender in payment of all debts," with limited exceptions. Everyone had to accept them whether they wanted to or not. Creditors sued, and at first, the Supreme Court agreed with them. In Hepburn v. Griswold (1870), the Court held that forcing a creditor to accept paper instead of the gold specified in a contract violated the Constitution. Ironically, the author of the opinion striking down legal tender—Chief Justice Salmon P. Chase—had been Lincoln's Treasury Secretary who helped launch the Greenbacks in the first place.

But the "victory" was short-lived. Within a year, President Ulysses S. Grant appointed two new justices, and the Court promptly reversed itself in *Knox v. Lee and Parker v. Davis (1871)*, the core of what historians call the Legal Tender Cases. Paper money was back, now wrapped in the authority of the Court. The reversal did more than restore Greenbacks; it signaled that the judiciary would permit Congress to do by emergency what the text did not clearly authorize. And the creep did not stop there. In *Juilliard v. Greenman (1884)*, the Court extended the doctrine, upholding paper legal tender not only in wartime but in peacetime too. From that point forward, the legal foundation for fiat was not a specific constitutional grant but a judicial permission slip.

Supporters of the status quo will answer that the Necessary and Proper Clause fills the gap; that declaring paper legal tender is "incidental" to Congress's power to borrow and regulate the currency. But that theory collapses under the history the framers actually lived. At the Constitutional Convention, the draft text briefly included a congressional power to "emit bills" (paper). The clause was struck after heated debate, with framers like Madison recording clear distrust of paper emissions. Whatever else "necessary and proper" might cover, it's a stretch to say it silently resurrects a power the Convention pointedly refused to grant.

Seen together, the legal story runs like this: Congress improvised Greenbacks under the pressure of war; the Supreme Court first said "no," then—with new appointments—said "yes," and later said "yes even in peacetime." The people were left with the appearance of constitutionality rather than the substance of it. And the broader constitutional pattern, visible in cases like *Barron*, shows how easily the plain text gets bent when it stands in the way of political necessity. The Constitution was meant to bind the government in chains. The Legal Tender Cases are the moment those chains were loosened.

This kind of pivot wasn't unique to money. For decades, the Supreme Court had also insisted that most of the Constitution's guarantees constrained only the federal government, not the states. In *Barron v. Baltimore (1833)*, the Court held that the Bill of Rights did not apply to state action. The result was a two-tiered system: lofty federal promises on paper, and state-level realities that often ignored them. Only after the Fourteenth Amendment—and then gradually, case by case through the twentieth century—did the Court begin "incorporating" core rights against the states, with full effect not really felt until the 1960s–1970s. The point isn't to relitigate those cases here, but to illustrate a pattern you see again in the Legal Tender saga: when the text restrains government, the government finds a way around the text—often with the courts' help.

The Moral Dimension

The framers of the Constitution were not theorizing in the dark. They had lived through the chaos of the Continental Congress issuing "Continentals," paper notes that inflated until they were worthless. Farmers and soldiers were left holding scraps of paper that could not buy bread. The phrase "not worth a Continental" became a bitter joke, a reminder that when governments can print at will, the people pay in poverty.

The lesson was simple: money must be real. It must be something of value, not a promise easily broken. The legal tender clause wasn't an accident. It was deliberate, hard-earned wisdom. They knew governments and bankers always look for shortcuts, and the temptation to issue paper money is irresistible. By prohibiting the states from doing it, and by not granting the federal government that power at all, the framers created a system of honest money that they hoped would last.

But they missed one critical point that they could not have foreseen at the time. The problem was not that legal tender laws coerced people to use bad money. The problem was that they assumed the ability to coerce anyone to use any particular money at all. Legal tender in and of itself is a violation of the free market – people's right to choose their own money.

Legal tender laws were never needed for gold or silver, because the metals were already valuable. If someone made a contract in Federal Reserve Notes, but someone offered to pay them in gold, they likely wouldn't have complained. Legal tender laws are usually put in place when the government starts printing funny money. They are there to force people to accept what they otherwise might not. Why not? Because they don't perceive it as valuable.

From the Roman Empire to early America, people could actually be jailed for refusing to accept the government's increasingly devalued money. This was necessary because the government could only profit from devalued money if the money was still accepted at full value. Whether they were shaving coins, diluting the metals with less valuable metals, or just printing at will, the tendency would be for people to accept lesser money at lesser value. Legal tender laws prevented that.

What good is printing money if it's worthless? How can you make it valuable? By forcing people to accept it.

Think about it: If you made a contract with someone to be paid in something very specific that you wanted, and they came to pay you with something else, what would you do? If it was something you saw as more valuable, you might take it. You wouldn't need a law to force you to accept it. If it was something you saw as less valuable, you might reject it. But legal tender might force you to accept it or face jail time.

Legal tender was the solution to bad money, and isn't really needed for good money. The legal tender clauses in the Constitution were not there to protect gold or silver. They were there to prevent states from forcing people to accept bad money.

Keep in mind, paper redeemable in gold or silver is often still treated as gold or silver itself. It's the same way you can pay someone with a check redeemable for $100, and it's regarded the same as if you gave them $100 in Federal Reserve Notes.

Sometimes, like with the Romans, people would set aside the good money. They'd hold on to the unshaved and unmixed coins and spend only the less valuable coins. This again gave extra value to the older coins, making the newer ones seem less valuable. This couldn't be allowed, and so anti-hoarding laws were created. Many governments have implemented this throughout history, including in the United States. Legal tender laws would then devalue the full coins as they had to be accepted at the same value as any other coin.

If laws were in effect today only making gold and silver legal tender, we would still have broken contracts that were made in crypto or other currencies. With vague language, they might even be able to make only certain gold or silver coins legal tender. This could give an ounce of gold minted by the federal government more value than an ounce of gold in its raw form or created by a private mint.

We might disagree with this interpretation, but who are we to stop the federal government from imposing its will on us by force?

Legal tender laws flip the natural order of money on its head. In a free market, people choose what to accept. If paper has value, it's because it can be redeemed for something real. Legal tender removes that choice. It commands: "You must take this, whether it holds value or not."

Who benefits? Debtors. And who is the biggest debtor in the world? The United States government. By enforcing paper tender, Washington ensures that every debt — including trillions in Treasury bonds — can be repaid in depreciated dollars. It is legalized theft from every saver, worker, and retiree whose stored value melts year after year.

Imagine you loaned your neighbor ten ounces of gold and he repaid you in Monopoly money. You'd call the sheriff. But with legal tender laws, the sheriff and the courts would tell you that you have to take that monopoly money because it's legal tender.

Some point to Texas' recognition of gold and silver as legal tender as a step forward. But federal supremacy nullifies it in practice. You can't pay federal taxes in gold, at least not without getting ripped off. Courts might not enforce contracts denominated in gold or silver if federal law overrides them. As long as Washington dictates that Federal Reserve Notes are the only ultimate tender, state experiments are symbolic at best.

Beyond the legal arguments lies the deeper question: what does it mean to force someone to accept paper in place of real payment? It is coercion. It is fraud with the seal of law. If two parties cannot freely decide what medium of exchange to use, they are not free. Legal tender laws are no different from laws forcing you to accept counterfeit bills at face value. The only difference is who prints them.

The Confusion of Government Coins

Most of the government coins today are not worth much. At times when inflation and the market prices of the metals make it more expensive to produce than the value of the coin, they look for cheaper ways to make them. Quarters used to contain silver until the cost of making the coin was more than a quarter of a dollar. Even pennies used to contain 95% copper, with just a little bit of zinc to make them harder. Today, with inflation, copper is far more valuable. So the coins are made with a copper plated zinc core, now containing only 2.5% copper. We don't usually think of copper as a precious metal, but there is an entire market dedicated to collecting scrap copper. In large volumes, it's very valuable.

So what about silver dollars? The government still makes silver dollars. These are made of one ounce of pure silver. But these are not the same silver dollars that our parents and grandparents used to collect. These contain more silver and contain more value in the metals than the older ones. Older ones can still be worth more as collector's items.

The government also still makes gold coins ranging in size from 1/10th ounce to one ounce, and with face values of $5 to $50 respectively. But why do these new gold and silver coins cost so much more to make than their face values?

These coins are typically made for collectors. There is a long legal and political history of why these are still made, but it creates some very interesting opportunities and problems.

These coins have a face value substantially less than the cost to produce. That means a silver coin with a $1 face value is worth about 1/40th of the metal it contains, and a $50 gold coin is worth about 1/80th of the gold it contains. Why would they do that to these coins when they do the opposite for their other coins? Because these coins are not circulated.

While these coins are legal tender at face value, the government will not spend them. In fact, they are prohibited by law. We can find this in the U.S. Code:

> 31 U.S. Code § 5118(b) The United States Government may not pay out any gold coin. A person lawfully holding United States coins and currency may present the coins and currency to the Secretary of the Treasury for exchange (dollar for dollar) for other United States coins and currency (other than gold and silver coins) that may be lawfully held. The Secretary shall make the exchange under regulations prescribed by the Secretary.

So what does that tell us? First, this is their escape clause. This law was first introduced in 1934, shortly after the executive order to make it illegal to hold gold. The U.S. was already trying to get out of its obligation to fulfill its promises of its gold and silver certificates. Before this law, if you had a certificate from the government, you could take it to the treasury, and they would give you the gold or silver. After this law, they could only give you Federal Reserve notes, which had already been established as legal tender.

This also means that if you brought them a $50 gold coin and asked for change, they would give you Federal Reserve notes.

We talk about people going to the treasury to redeem these, but in reality, that's not how it works. Larger banks and institutions would be the ones to take your deposits to the treasury and make exchanges in large amounts. Knowing how the treasury would behave, local banks would collect these notes under the same rules.

Similar to every other time weak money was forced into use by legal tender laws, good money like these gold and silver coins were forced out of circulation. Instead of being used as money, they are hoarded by collectors and those preparing for the collapse of the Fed.

While you might outsmart the treasury and refuse to take in your gold and silver coins for FRNs, you could still be potentially affected by this. If the government seizes these coins from you, they would only be obligated to repay you at face value. This has even been tested where an individual sent a

1 ounce silver eagle to pay his taxes. The IRS credited his account by only $1, though the silver content was worth much more.

But there's an upside to this. There are laws that prohibit carrying items more than $10,000 internationally without declaring them and paying taxes. There's a whole other interesting topic of why so many countries set this at the same $10,000 USD and not some other amount in their own currency. Individuals carrying more than $10,000 worth of gold have been told by U.S. customs that they can only value the coins at face value. $10,000 in $50 coins is 200 coins. At about $4,000 per coin, that's about $800k you can now travel with internationally.

I know this scenario probably doesn't mean anything to most people, but it has been tested in another way. One man decided to pay his employees in gold coins. At the time, they were worth closer to $2,000. He would pay his employees in these coins every other week, and declare on their taxes that they received $50. This actually did hold up in court.

Unfortunately, because the government really wanted to punish them, they were able to successfully charge him with money laundering. Money laundering typically requires that the government show they were hiding the source of money from illegal sources. In this case, they were able to convict anyway. The angle was that the business owner was buying these coins for about $2000 and paying them to his employees. His employees would then go to a pawn shop and exchange them for $2000 in FRNs.

Had this case had more national attention, I don't think the money laundering charges would have stuck. But money laundering is one of those ham sandwich laws – laws which many attorneys agree could be used to convict a ham sandwich. It means that these laws are so broad, they make it easy for prosecutors to convict innocent people. Follow these examples at your own risk.

The Way Forward

Ending the Fed requires ending the fraud of legal tender. That doesn't mean waiting for Congress or the courts to confess their sins. It means individuals and communities must choose alternatives now. Gold and silver contracts, crypto exchanges, local barter systems — all of these are acts of defiance that chip away at the monopoly.

Every time you trade outside the Fed's paper system, you withdraw a little bit of your consent. Enough withdrawals, and the system collapses. That was true in 1776, and it is true today.

There's one important piece of information that often goes overlooked. The law that makes Federal Reserve Notes legal tender can be found in 31 U.S.C. 5103:

```
United States coins and currency (including
Federal reserve notes and circulating notes of
Federal reserve banks and national banks) are
legal tender for all debts, public charges,
taxes, and dues. Foreign gold or silver coins
are not legal tender for debts.
```

Notice that it says you can pay your debts with this money. It does not say that you have to accept this money as payment for any transaction. This is an important distinction. Some people believe that if they open a shop, they would have to accept U.S. currency or that they are prohibited from accepting precious metals or crypto. This simply isn't true.

It is true that if you agree to sell something to someone for an ounce of gold to be paid at a later time, they could discharge that debt with Federal Reserve Notes. But there is nothing preventing you from making that agreement. You can even cancel the offer or agreement before you hand over the goods, if you see the buyer is not intending to pay in the currency you demand.

Picture selling a car. You can agree to sell the car for a certain price in gold. If you haven't signed over the title, and the buyer fails to deliver the gold, you can call it off at any time.

I'm not saying you should refuse to accept Federal Reserve Notes. Doing so would significantly reduce your pool of potential customers, and trading those notes for gold, silver, or crypto is fairly simple. If anything, you might want to simply offer a discount for anyone paying in better currencies, or a penalty for paying in FRNs.

Crash The Fed

Whatever Goes Up Must Come Down

On money in general, I'd like to make a quick note - no pun intended. Many people have different theories about what gives money its value. You need to look no further than promises. Money, or currency, is simply a promise.

Stories are often told about how, before the notes we have today, we had gold certificates, before that we had real gold coins, and before that we had barter. This skips a very important step.

Between barter and gold, there were notes. The idea was that if you wanted to barter with me, but you wanted to offer a crop that you wouldn't harvest until later in the year, you would write me a note. That note would be redeemable in the future. This was the first money – a promise, printed from thin air. When this promise was redeemed, it would be destroyed.

Imagine an apple farmer creates an IOU for a bag of apples, and uses that to buy some meat for his family. Eventually, someone will bring that IOU back to the farmer in exchange for his apples. The farmer now holds an IOU that he created himself, promising a bag of apples from himself. It has already been redeemed. It is now worthless. If he wants to eat some of his own apples, he doesn't need any money to do so. He could give it to someone else to buy some more meat, but that would be making a new promise. It's creating a new debt to someone else. He could just as easily create a new one. He could create a thousand of them, but he might end up with a lot of upset people demanding apples he can't produce. It's the same thing that happens when people make promises they can't keep.

The Fed creates money in the same way. The government issues an IOU in the form of a bond – a promise. The Fed then issues an IOU in the form of a FRN back to the government – another promise. When the government pays off its debt by taking back one of the IOUs from the Fed, the Fed also pays off its debt by taking back one of the FRNs from the government. It's a system of two promises with perceived value that both create value for each other, and cancel each other out.

This gets more complicated, of course, because of fractional reserve lending, but these are derivative promises based on other promises. The government takes these FRNs and spends them. They make their way through the economy and are deposited into a bank. The bank then deposits its money with the Fed. The Fed is now holding both of the promises, and leveraging its own promises to create new promises. But this doesn't change the basic principle that when one IOU is redeemed for another, they both cancel out and must be destroyed.

If the government were to buy back its bonds with FRNs, and the Fed were allowed to keep those FRNs to spend or loan, then there would have been no point in issuing the bonds in the first place. The notes themselves are backed by the bonds, and the bonds are backed by the FRNs. If one is destroyed, the other must be destroyed. Otherwise, the government would have given a private bank a full license to print as much money as they want without any oversight at all. Though they have nearly done this, there are still restrictions.

It is said that whatever goes up, must dome down. Like the apple farmer creating promises out of thin air, eventually the value of those promises is destroyed. Either the promises are redeemed or he can't deliver. In either case, the promises are worthless. The Fed is no different. If the government pays off its promises, any money backed by those promises becomes worthless. If the government can't pay off its promises, they also become worthless.

The Myth of the Benevolent Gold Standard

Whenever the failures of fiat money are exposed, the default solution many propose is simple: "Bring back the gold standard." At first glance, it makes sense. Gold is real. It cannot be printed by decree. For centuries, it served as the foundation of honest trade.

First, I want to make a distinction that often goes overlooked. People often use the term "gold standard" to mean money that is backed by gold. Though there is often some overlap, that is not always the case. Gold certificates are paper certificates that are backed by gold, usually in a specific amount. No law can change that. It's a contract with the bank. Someone deposits gold into a bank, and the bank issues a note so that person can take that same amount of gold right back out. He can also use this certificate as money, and anyone else can redeem that money. U.S. Treasury bills used to say some variation of "redeemable by the bearer on demand in silver". Certain bills were either backed by gold or silver.

The gold standard represents a different paradigm, where a certain number of dollars was equal to a certain amount of gold or silver. Today, we can buy gold or silver in a market where the price fluctuates constantly. When there was a gold standard, the price would be fixed – at least it was fixed if you were buying from the U.S. Treasury.

Though these are similar concepts and often overlap, they are not the same. The difference is critical. With a gold standard, the standard can always be changed, just as easily as it was created. But it never means that the government has enough gold for all of its notes to be redeemed, and it doesn't mean that they aren't going to be printing like crazy. In fact, when Nixon killed the gold standard in 1971, it was because they had been printing money, and there wasn't enough gold to be redeemed at $35 per ounce. Instead of admitting they had a problem by increasing the price, they stopped selling their gold altogether.

But the problem with our money isn't whether or not the Treasury will sell their gold at a fixed price, or whether they hold enough gold for everyone to redeem their notes. It doesn't matter if there is a gold standard or a gold backing. If the same political class that corrupted paper money is given the authority to set a standard, the result is inevitable: manipulation, suspension, and betrayal. History proves it.

A government-run gold standard is not a safeguard against tyranny. It is merely a different leash — one that will be cut the moment it becomes inconvenient to those in power.

Private banks have also tried issuing their own gold certificates, and often those fail for the same reason. But a truly free system would mean that any bank could issue their own certificates, and the best would become the most popular. Those who opened their books to third party auditors who could make physical examinations of the gold would likely have the highest degree of trust, and the most customers. Banks without this safeguard would leave people skeptical. Insurance could also be available, further strengthening consumer confidence, and insurance companies would likely demand regular audits to limit their risk.

Other banks might openly lend their gold by printing more certificates, but pay their depositors with interest. They might publish their reserve rates so people stay confident in using their banks. This might be limited to high net-worth individuals with money to invest in high risk accounts, but there's certainly no reason it should be outlawed.

There are already organizations issuing gold backed cryptocurrencies, which allow people to trade "certificates" anonymously through blockchain technology. In fact, there are other organizations issuing FRN backed cryptocurrencies, which are directly redeemable in U.S. Dollars. Many people hold this currency so that they have assets in the blockchain, but they are protected from the volatility of other markets.

The same problem exists with both of these types of organizations. They have a particular asset in store, either FRNs or gold. When they add more FRNs or gold into their vaults, they have to be able to issue new coins or tokens to represent those new holdings. When someone cashes in that currency for FRNs or gold, the coins or tokens must be destroyed.

Because the issuing organization ultimately has absolute control over the creation and destruction of these currencies, there is nothing to stop them from over issuing. In fact, any organization that claims to have billions of FRNs backing their virtual asset is simply stating that metaphorically. Nobody is holding billions of FRNs in a vault. If anything they are using other banks to store their assets. Some have been accused of using their bank deposits to buy treasuries from the government, causing them to create more debt. While this might indicate that some of these companies aren't perfect, the government's war on cryptocurrencies has ensured that there is little competition.

Some would argue that the government has a moral obligation to be better than any for-profit or private entity, but history shows that's not the case. Just look at the history of the dollar going from a gold and silver backing to absolute fiat. If the government wanted to create its own currency, I don't see any reason why they couldn't also compete in the same market. Anyone who wants to trust their money could do so freely. But creating a monopoly where they are the only choice is criminal, and it further gives them the ability to destroy its value without the consequence of a boycott of their worthless product.

Gold is valuable not because it is decreed by government, but because it is scarce, durable, and trusted. Its strength comes from markets choosing it, not governments mandating it.

The framers were right to insist on gold and silver as tender. But they also lived in a world where alternatives were limited. Today, we have Bitcoin, privacy coins, local currencies, barter networks — tools the framers never dreamed of. The principle remains the same: money must be outside the control of the state.

A true gold standard is not government-managed convertibility. It is you and I freely choosing to trade in gold when we want, without permission, without coercion, and without confiscation.

Gold has a role. It will always hold value. But the solution is broader: freedom of currency. The right to use gold, silver, Bitcoin, or barter — without legal tender laws, without government monopolies, without coercion.

The myth of the benevolent gold standard is that government can be trusted to restrain itself. The reality is that only individuals, free to choose, can restrain government by refusing its paper.

The real gold standard is voluntary exchange. Everything else is fraud dressed in yellow.

The Fed's Perpetual Debt Machine

If you've ever looked for a safe way to save your money, increase your income, or build wealth, then you have no doubt heard about passive income. The idea is that you set up a certain business that mostly operates itself, and you get checks every month for doing almost nothing. This could be in the form of owning a business that someone else operates, buying a rental property, or investing in stocks that pay dividends.

People like these investments because if you're fortunate enough to have enough of them, you can live a pretty nice life, quit your day job, and provide abundance for your family. If you have the means, it's really a no-brainer.

Some will debate the morality of such businesses, claiming that nobody should benefit from the labor of others. The other side of that will claim that your investment capital is a risk that creates opportunity for someone else to make money. The morality certainly depends on the system itself, as there are plenty of ways to set up passive income, some more unethical than others.

Lending money creates passive income through interest. Again, many will claim that lending money at all is immoral – usury is banned by the Old Testament. To most people, what makes the difference between moral and immoral lending is whether it's possible to pay off the debt.

Lending someone $500 and asking them to make 6 payments of $100 doesn't seem like such a crime. On the other hand, predatory credit card companies actively seeking to lend people more than they can handle is criminal. Some of these companies will set high limits and interest rates such that the borrower at some point can only make the minimum payments. This can easily turn $1,000 borrowed into $5,000 repaid several years later. It's easy to point blame at the borrower for not being responsible with their line of credit. But the banks that lend this money are brilliant financial gurus who understand the numbers. They know that if they give $5,000 credit cards to people with a certain credit history, they will more than double their money. They know that even though some percent of those people will bail on their debt and never pay it back, the others will more than compensate for the loss. And they know exactly what percent that is.

Lending money might not be unethical on its own, but knowingly preying on the financially illiterate is criminal. Keeping people in perpetual debt creates passive income.

Enter the Federal Reserve.

If you wanted to design a system that would place an entire nation in perpetual debt, a system that ensured every child was born owing you their labor, you could not have built anything better than the Federal Reserve. It is not a "stabilizer," as it claims, nor a "guardian of prosperity." It is a debt machine, and it runs with mathematical precision.

Most people believe debt is an accident — the result of bad budgeting or irresponsible spending. But under the Fed, debt is structural. It is not just common, it is inevitable. The way our money is created ensures that every dollar comes into existence as a debt, and that more is always owed than exists.

Some believe that the Federal Reserve prints money out of thin air, but if that were the case, there would be no debt. The government would just print what it needs and spend it, not owing anything to anyone. Instead, the government prints money that is backed by debt. All the money they print is associated with treasury bonds that are given to the Federal Reserve. If they don't issue those bonds, they can't print the money.

It gets even shadier when you realize that the government pays for the ink, paper and labor, and holds and operates the printing machines in the Bureau of Engraving and Printing. The Federal Reserve doesn't even print the money, they just authorize the government to use their name.

Earlier U.S. money was backed by gold or silver. The notes actually said on them that they were "redeemable to the bearer on demand" for gold or silver. But when the U.S. went off the gold standard (and also the silver standard), what was the money backed by? They are still "notes", which are financial instruments like IOUs. What gives them their value is the fact that they can be redeemed. But where can you redeem them and for what?

Because FRNs are issued by the Federal Reserve, they can be redeemed at the Federal Reserve for U.S. Treasury Bonds. But this is not an obligation they have to just anyone. The fact that you are holding a FRN means that the Fed owes you money. But try to take it to the Fed to cash out and they'll just pay you what they owe you in the same FRNs. This is legal because of the legal tender laws.

Just as those bonds are created in parallel with the notes they back, when the bonds are repaid, both the bonds and the notes must be destroyed. This keeps the balance sheet balanced. If the government issues $1 million in bonds, they can print $1 million in notes. The money supply is then expanded by fractional reserve lending, but the core money supply is matched one-to-one with the bonds.

That is, until interest is added. The trick is that the bonds pay interest. Imagine the government prints $1 million in bonds and then $1 million in notes. Some time later, the bonds might be worth $1.1 million, a ten percent increase. They didn't go up in value, that's just the terms of the bond contract, to repay the holder with interest. If the government wanted to pay off their debt, they would have to buy those $1.1 million in bonds with $1.1 million in notes. But when the notes were created, there were only $1 million. That means there is not enough money to pay off the government's debt.

Just like the predatory credit card companies that want customers who are in perpetual debt, the Federal Reserve has designed the perfect system where it is mathematically, literally, and physically impossible to pay off the debt. This is not just how they make a profit, but how they have locked in their customers from ever leaving.

The fixed one-to-one relationship is the basis of all the money, but there are derivative ways the money supply and debt can further expand independently. The government gets its FRNs and spends them into circulation. Instead of borrowing more money from the Fed, they can borrow from the public, by selling bonds to the public. Because this is the issue of more debt without the issue of new FRNs, the government's debt expands. When the buyers return to collect on what is owed, the bonds are destroyed, but the FRNs are not. That is because these bonds were not the basis for creation of new FRNs.

Similarly, if these FRNs are deposited into banks, they can be lent back out. These FRNs now appear in two different bank accounts, both the original account where it was deposited, and in the account of a person it was lent to. In fact, it can appear in many accounts, with many factors determining how many places it can be at the same time. There is often a physical or abstract note created as a debt instrument used to allow the money to be copied into another account. Similar to the creation of money against treasury bonds, when the loans are repaid, both the notes and the copied money are destroyed.

We've just looked at three systems for creating debt and money. The first is where money and debt are created together. The second is where the government takes on more debt by issuing bonds to get back already issued money. The third is where the money supply expands by banks lending already existing money. In all of these cases, the only real producer of money is the government by printing bonds. Those bonds are debt.

Proponents of the Federal Reserve will say that because a lot of the debt is created by selling bonds to the public, the debt can be repaid. They believe the government could tax $1 million out of the economy, and use that to buy back $1 million of its bonds, reducing its debt by the same amount. That money would then be back in the public's hands. Eventually it would be taxed again, and the government could buy back another $1 million in debt, until there is no debt left. While this is certainly possible with bonds that were sold to the public, this is not possible with bonds that were given to the Fed as the basis for creating new FRNs. When those bonds are repaid, the FRNs must be destroyed, and will not reenter the economy. If this weren't the case, there would be no point in issuing the bonds in the first place.

As of 2025, there are about $2.32 trillion in FRNs floating around the world. The Federal Reserve reports they are holding more than $4 trillion in treasury bonds. The total national debt is closer to $40 trillion. The government could tax and pay off most of that debt by buying back all of its public bonds, but in the end, they would still be left with that $4 trillion. If they collected all $2.32 trillion in FRNs and gave it all to the Fed, it would game over. The government would still owe about $1.7 trillion to the Fed, and there would be no money in existence at all.

If the Fed holds bonds that are only redeemable for FRNs, why would they hold these bonds at all? Why would they ever need to redeem them for FRNs when they can just print whatever they want? Why doesn't the government just print their bonds directly and make them legal tender, without involving a private bank? There may be constitutional arguments against that, but those are the same arguments against the current system with the Fed. This is not about printing money from thin air, this is about controlling the government with debt. The interest is the secret to making the debt unpayable.

Why can't they pay off the debt with something else, like gold? All the world's estimated 210,000 metric tons of gold ever mined is only worth about $23 trillion. Little of that actually belongs to the government. They'd have to steal it if they ever wanted a fighting chance at paying off that debt. But since the debt is denominated in dollars, not gold, the government would still have to negotiate a payoff with the Fed. This would be bankruptcy.

Who would want this? The Fed has an infinite flow of passive income from the federal government, paid for with taxes that a private bank couldn't collect without the help of the government. Politicians have an endless supply of money for their projects, and power to control their enemies and create more wealth. It doesn't make sense for anyone involved to get rid of this debt. This isn't a broken system. This is a system working exactly as it was designed. The only people in a position to end the system are the ones who benefit the most. The system has created a perverse incentive for those tasked with ending it to continue feeding it.

Debt is Slavery

Many people, even those who want to end the Fed, get very uncomfortable about the statement that debt is slavery. Let's look at a few facts.

1. The federal debt can not be paid, it can only be serviced.
2. Servicing the debt can be done by printing new money, but that causes inflation.
3. Inflation can be reduced by increasing taxes to service the debt.
4. The government is the first spender of all new money.
5. If your savings are inflated away, you have to earn more money downstream from what the government spends.
6. If you own property that is taxed, you must earn money downstream from what the government spends.

If slavery is the extraction of labor from people who don't want to work for you, inflation and other taxes force people to work for the government, directly or indirectly. Nobody is free to abandon society and live off the land within a smaller community. They are forced to contribute to the national economy, whether they like it or not. Even the Amish are forced to pay taxes.

It's easy to list the differences. None are held in captivity, and few are beaten to be kept in line. But those barbaric practices were not the purpose of slavery. They were simply the means to an end of extracting labor from people.

Instead of forcing people to work to avoid being whipped, they force people to work to avoid punishment for not paying taxes. They even make some of these tax slaves feel guilty, by telling them they are working to pay off a debt that they never signed for. We're not just talking *all* taxes here. Some taxes, especially excises, could be said to be voluntary. The consumer gets something directly in return. Although this is more avoidable than direct taxes, it is still violence. Direct taxes on land are unavoidable. Even those who are too poor to own their own homes pay a property tax that's built into their rent, and makes it harder for them to escape the rent cycle and buy a house.

In recent years, the national deficit has been around $1 trillion. In 2024 it rose to $2 trillion. About $1.3 trillion of that is spent servicing the debt – that means interest only payments. About $2.4 trillion was collected from individuals in income tax. There are many ways to look at these numbers. What I like to point out is that eliminating debt interest would have almost eliminated the deficit in recent years. In 2024, it would have eliminated about half of it. Half of everything that individuals pay in income tax goes directly to banks and investors who lent their money to the government.

If you've ever had to put in extra hours or get a second job just to make ends meet, you understand how this system forces us to work harder. This is why politicians always focus on getting as close as possible to a 0% unemployment rate. They hate idle hands, just like the typical slave owner.

Many speak about unfunded liabilities, these are future promises to pay something. This differs from the national debt because the money hasn't been borrowed or spent yet. The actual amount that will need to be spent is unknown, but unfunded liabilities help to ensure that expenses stay high. About 36% of the federal expenses every year go to Social Security and Medicare. These are the unfunded liabilities. But there is more to the story. Social Security is a literal Ponzi scheme, and the federal government's protectionism of the healthcare industry helps the industry increase profits. That means that most of what Medicare spends is simply the government subsidizing an industry whose profits they already helped to inflate. It's a double-edged sword. Protectionism has placed healthcare out of reach for many, forcing them to rely on Medicare. By eliminating protectionism, prices will fall naturally to be affordable to everyone, without government assistance.

The government also plays a game with debt ceilings, or a maximum total debt that the government can borrow. This is nothing more than theatrics. When they vote to borrow more money, all they have to do is vote to raise the debt ceiling. The debt ceiling has been raised 22 times in the last 30 years. The last time an increase was voted down was back in 2011, and it has been increased 11 times since. The increased debt ceiling is usually passed in the same bill that allocates the annual budget. It appears they can raise the debt ceiling just as easily as the debt itself, so there is really no point in having a ceiling at all.

The Illusion of Prosperity

When the Fed expands credit, people feel richer. Housing prices boom, stock prices soar, governments hand out stimulus checks. But it is borrowed prosperity. It feels like we are richer than ever – more people own cars and houses, and buy new ones even when they don't really need to. Every household has a refrigerator, flat screen TV, and likely a microwave, electric washing machine and dryer… all of these things are becoming more high-tech with lots of bells and whistles.

But our wealth is not increasing in the way that we think it is. Household debt in 2025 is $18 trillion, according to the Federal Reserve. An average of about $105,000 per household. Many of those people will die before their debts are paid off, and the banks still turn a profit even factoring in debts that they'll never collect. More people have big fancy houses, but little equity. They are still living paycheck to paycheck, at risk of losing everything overnight.

But how can we not be wealthy if we have more today than kings had a century ago? While most of these things seem valuable, they aren't. A century ago, few people had automobiles. Although the industrial revolution enabled mass production, only about 4.5 million vehicles were manufactured in 1925. Each year, more than 90 million cars are produced worldwide, and that's with sales slowing down because so many people already have cars, and prices are going up from inflation.

It would be difficult to calculate the actual cost of production. Manpower is required to extract raw materials from the earth, refine them, form them, create parts, transport them back and forth across the country, and finally assemble them into a car. We know that in the factory, it would take about 97 man-hours in 1918, 51 hours in 1923, and as little as 20 hours in 2025.

As technology advances, it takes fewer people less time to produce these things. While inflation makes us think that cars are expensive today at $50,000 while they used to only cost $300, the truth is that the cost of making a car has decreased substantially. They are now made from lighter materials, and include computerized everything, anti-lock brakes, airbags, and strategically engineered frames that make them lighter, more efficient and safer. These are things that weren't available a hundred years ago, no matter how wealthy you were.

And when we buy those cars today, a lot more profit is going to the bank than the manufacturer compared to a century ago.

The same goes for housing. Lighter but stronger materials are cheaper than before, and they are designed where a small group of people can build an entire neighborhood seemingly overnight.

So if things are less expensive today than they were before, why are people struggling so hard? Banks have inserted themselves into all of these industries with the promises of inflating profits for the manufacturers and sellers. It used to be that if you walked into a car dealership and told them you were going to pay cash, they'd be happy. Not anymore. Now salesmen get a cash incentive from the bank for each loan sold. They are more interested in selling loans than cars. Since this has become the norm, people expect to get a loan when they buy a new car. Whatever they say they can afford, the bank will work backwards to get them the biggest loan they can afford. The dealer then takes this number and sells them a car right at the top of their price range. The same goes for housing with realtors.

All of these specialized loans flood the market with money, ensuring that anyone selling anything can turn down a lowball offer, knowing some fool will come along soon ready to pay whatever the bank tells them they can afford. This further drives up prices, and it's all backed by the Fed. The more we are in debt, the more money the banks make. Loan terms keep getting longer and longer, ensuring the banks can increase consumer debt, and increase their profits. These loans used to be risky, but the Federal Reserve and special government programs now cover the risk.

It's the same game. Whether the debt belongs to the government or to us, more debt means more profit for the banks and the Federal Reserve. It makes us think we are getting wealthier, while the net worth of many Americans is going further into the red. People below what is considered the poverty line in third world countries have a higher net worth than many Americans.

Inflation Is A One-Way Street

Who doesn't want lower prices? If printing more money causes prices to go up, couldn't we just deflate the currency and make prices come down?

There are a lot of problems with deflation, and the people who suffer the most are the borrowers. With inflation, while prices go up, money becomes easier to get. You can either increase your prices or money might be easier to borrow. While it might feel like there's never enough money because of increasing prices, there's actually more circulation – and that's *why* the prices are higher.

With more money in circulation, loans are easier to pay. Those dollars are worth less, which means the banks are getting back less than they gave you. Don't feel bad for them. They already knew this was coming and made their interest rates far higher than inflation.

But with deflation, less money in circulation means it's harder to get that money. That means it's harder to pay off your loans. More people will default on their loans and the banks will seize the underlying assets.

It also hurts businesses. Think about a company that makes a product. They might have used credit to buy $1 million worth of source materials, parts or ingredients. If they bought that on credit, they would have a debt of $1 million. Now if the money supply evaporates, and prices are forced to fall, the business still has to sell their products for a higher price to pay off the loan. If prices fall too far too fast, they will go bankrupt and have to shut down their business. That creates unemployment, and now these people will have to find new jobs that pay less and have the same trouble with any loans they have taken out for their homes.

The Only Way Out

There is no reform that makes perpetual debt sustainable. Balanced budgets, spending caps, "responsible" Fed chairs — all theater. The only way out is to crash the machine and eliminate the debt. That does not mean chaos for us — it means chaos for them. For us, it means freedom to build parallel systems, to trade outside their paper racket, to reclaim the honest money the framers intended.

History teaches that every fiat system ends the same: debasement, collapse, reset. The only question is whether we will be victims of the crash, or prepared architects of what comes next.

Part II
The Illusion of Political Solutions

> The constitution has either authorized such a
> government as we have had, or has been
> powerless to prevent it.
> — Lysander Spooner

Why Voting Won't Save Us

Every four years, Americans line up at the polls believing they are choosing the direction of the country. Candidates promise change, reform, and accountability. "If we just elect the right people," we are told, "things will get better."

But when it comes to the Federal Reserve, the truth is simple: **voting will not save us.** The system is designed to ensure it never makes it onto the ballot in any meaningful way.

For years, activists rallied around Ron Paul's *Audit the Fed* bill. It was supposed to be the first step — shine a light on the Fed's books, expose the corruption, and then reform would follow.

In 2010, the Dodd Frank bill was passed which caused a brief audit of the Fed, but all this did was show how much they lent to foreign banks and private institutions. It was limited, and left most of the End the Fed crowd still looking like conspiracy theorists.

In 2012, Ron Paul's End the Fed bill passed the house but died in the Senate where it wasn't even put on the floor for a vote. This is a typical way that bills are killed by individuals or a small committee that controls the voting calendar in both the federal and state legislatures.

In 2015 and 2016, Rand Paul was pushing another Audit the Fed bill that was even supported by Bernie Sanders. Of course, Sanders wasn't interested in a full audit and ultimately withdrew his support when it came time to vote. The bill only got 52 out of the 60 votes needed and never passed. Rand Paul continued to introduce bills to audit the Fed, but none have passed.

Are our representatives just not interested in knowing what goes on at the biggest bank in the country? Do they not care how this bank is able to lend an unlimited amount of money to the government? Or do they know, and work hard to keep it a secret, so the rest of the world will never know?

To meaningfully "end the Fed" through Congress would require a majority in both houses and a president willing to sign it. That's only a few hundred people who need to support this bill. But think about all the projects that would be on the chopping block if an audit passed and momentum was gained to end the Fed. Do you believe that these politicians would turn their back on the bank that funds all their dream projects, and the promises that get them elected? Do you really believe that 218 members of the House, 60 senators, and a sitting president will simultaneously vote to strip away the very tool that funds their spending sprees?

The federal government depends on the Fed. Politicians love it because it lets them spend whatever they want. They can buy votes today and push the cost onto future generations. Expecting those same politicians to abolish their golden goose is fantasy.

The Left wants welfare. The Right wants the military. They both want Social Security and other programs the government can't really afford. They both rely on the Fed to paper over the difference.

Democrats will never risk losing their spending machine. Republicans will never risk losing theirs. Their fight is somewhere between a distraction from the real problem and a skirmish about how to spend the fake money.

No matter who wins elections, the Fed never shrinks. Under Bush, the Fed bailed out banks. Under Obama, it doubled down on quantitative easing. Under Trump, it cut rates to the floor. Under Biden, it expanded further. Different parties, same machine.

Clinton is credited with the most recent budget surplus, but this was only achieved with higher taxes. Year over year, spending has only gone down 5 times since 1965 – that's an average of once every ten years! But don't be confused, those still weren't cuts! Most of those drops are on years following massive one time expenses like bailing out banks or COVID programs.

Crash The Fed

Often we'll hear politicians talk about cutting budgets, but they are really just talking about reducing automatic increases – and even then, they are often still spending more than the previous year!

Even if some brave politician did make it to Washington with a plan to rein in the Fed, what then? The institutions themselves crush dissent. The banking lobby writes the laws. The Treasury and the Fed are staffed by the same insiders who bounce back and forth between Goldman Sachs, Citibank, and government posts. Others in both major parties have their campaigns bankrolled by major banks.

A freshman senator isn't going to dismantle that network. At best, they'll get a committee seat. At worst, they'll be sidelined, blackmailed, or bought.

Ron Paul ran for president three times, electrified millions, and put "End the Fed" on bumper stickers and protest signs across the nation. He sparked the strongest anti-Fed movement in modern history.

And what did the system do? It rigged debates to exclude him. It manipulated vote counts. The Republican National Committee changed rules mid-stream to block his delegates from even being seated at the convention.

If an honest man with mass support can't even get a fair vote counted, what does that tell you about the system? Voting is tolerated only as long as it doesn't threaten the core power structure.

The Fed protects politicians from accountability. Without it, they would have to raise taxes to fund wars, welfare, and pork. That would make them unpopular and unelectable. The Fed allows them to spend invisibly through inflation.

That's why ending the Fed is not up for a vote. It is not a "partisan issue." It is the foundation of the system itself. And no system votes to abolish itself.

This doesn't mean we should disengage from politics entirely. It means we should recognize its limits. Voting is like rearranging the chairs on the deck of the Titanic. It doesn't mend the damage made from an iceberg.

The real solution lies outside the ballot box in direct action. The Fed cannot be ended by majority vote. It can only be ended when enough people walk away, leaving the politicians with nothing left to inflate.

Ending The Fed By Legislation Is Tyranny

There's another odd paradox to consider when voting to end the Fed. Even if we could get enough legislators to agree that it needed to end, how would they do it?

Most who support ending the Fed are proponents of free markets, and against government regulation. In this light, de facto elimination of the Federal Reserve by legislation would be a complete act of tyranny. It's one thing to say that banks have to operate by certain standards, but it's another to single out one bank and tell them that they can no longer exist. The Federal Reserve, just like every other bank, has the right to exist and do business.

That statement has upset and confused many people, but bear with me. The Fed's mere existence doesn't give it power. In fact, their ability to print notes doesn't even give them power. Their power comes from their partnership with the federal government. Eliminate their special advantage by removing legal tender laws, and allow other banks to issue notes by whatever backing they like, and the Fed will be placed on equal footing with everyone else.

All banks collectively have a right to exist, partner with each other, and do many of the things we often hate them for. What they do not have the right to do is to commit fraud and force people to use their products. The legal ability to commit these crimes is granted through legislation and could be reversed through repeal, but that's not the only way.

If the Fed keeps doing what it's doing, it will put itself out of business. If they are forced to provide value to their customers as every other bank does, we could see those notes actually become worth something. We could even see an end of inflation or a gold backing. But legislating them out of existence would be an act of choosing winners and losers, the very thing that most advocates of ending the Fed claim to be against.

We should not sink to their level.

The Left-Right Divide as a Distraction

The left wants more welfare programs, and to take care of struggling workers. The right wants lower taxes. Or at least they say they do.

It's important to recognize that the paradigm of the left versus the right is not only a fabricated distraction, but it's so vague in its terms that it's virtually meaningless.

To say one side believes in something is a statement of generalization. It's prejudice. These are two large groups consisting of more than 100 million people each. They are not all the same. In both groups, there are also smaller groups. One group is the "loud minority," the ones who make all the noise, show up at protests, make demands, and make media appearances. Another small group within each are the politicians, the ones who actually make policy.

Then there is the largest group who are the voters, mostly politically inactive, being led and controlled by the first two groups. They don't all want the same thing. The loud minority often just wants attention. They create problems where there are none, just so they can have people look at them. They might do this for attention alone or for profit. The politicians are a little different. They'll say they want one thing, or that they'll fight for another, but at the end of the day, they are making secret deals for their own benefit. The descriptions of these groups are, of course, also generalizations.

While most Americans are different, we can distill what they all want down to one thing. They want to have a good life, to be left alone, to feel safe and comfortable where they live, to be able to afford the things they need, and to be able to enjoy life. There is no left and right between them. The left-right paradigm enters when the media and politicians tell them that in order to have what they want, there is only one way to get it. They are told who is standing in their way, and that they must support a political agenda in order to get what they want. The left is taught to hate the people and the programs on the right, and the right is taught to hate the people and programs on the left.

Politicians usually fail to deliver because they aren't interested in giving these things to people, and they know their plans will never solve anything. They only talk about these plans because it gets them elected.

In reality, we're all on the same side. It's not left versus right, it's freedom versus tyranny. And this all comes back to the Fed.

In order for the Fed to do its thing, it needs the government to continue to overspend. It needs people to keep surrendering all their labor in exchange for money fabricated from nothing. They can't do this if everyone has what they want. They need our struggle to fuel expenses.

It benefits the Fed for the government to have large spending and welfare programs. This makes up about a third of the government's budget. But they know that if this expanded any further, inflation could get out of control. So they convince the right to fight against this. Many on the right who have worked hard and built up a little wealth know that these programs will mean more taxes. It means that people on the left will benefit from the labor of the right. It's easy to see how these two groups can hate each other.

But what if that wasn't the only option? What if we all came to realize that the government shouldn't be brokering deals with money that doesn't belong to them. They shouldn't be stealing from anyone, and what they have already stolen should be returned to the people. There is no easy way to do this fairly. Most have been robbed through some sort of taxation. Others have had land and even lives stolen. This is already lost, and there is no easy way to compensate everyone, especially since the government doesn't have the money and some of those things are irreplaceable.

People often tell me they think the government should pay off its debts or at least cut spending before they start cutting taxes. But what would that do? If the government stopped spending money but continued to collect it, all the money would end up in the treasury. There would be none to circulate.

Money is economic power, and this would put all the economic power in the hands of the government.

But when that money is paid out of the treasury to people who have little, it's being returned to the people. It's the opposite of a tax. You may be jumping ahead and saying, "yeah, but that's money that was stolen from someone else." Really? I thought it was money that was created from nothing. You might say "yeah, but after it was created from nothing, I earned it, then it was taken from me." Well if you spent your life working for money that you knew was worthless, you should probably recognize that there is room for improvement in your economic behavior.

Let's also ask, do we have to take from those with money in order to pay for these programs? Some on the left are even starting to question why the government doesn't just print everything they need. MMT or Modern Monetary Theory teaches exactly that. Well, why not? Those who disagree with this will argue that if they cut taxes while printing money to pay for these programs, they are still stealing from everyone through inflation. Yes, but isn't that inevitable anyway? Is someone, somewhere, holding on to these dollars with the misled belief that they will go up in value? Only those who are dangerously misled, like those who invest in government bonds. We should all be divesting our wealth from dollars to anything more stable.

The most dangerous feature of the Left–Right divide is not just distraction. It is division. By keeping Americans at each other's throats, the ruling class ensures no united movement against the Fed can form.

If Left and Right realized they were both victims of the same theft, the system would collapse overnight. As we'll soon see, people on both sides can join forces to crash the Fed with direct action. But as long as they see each other as enemies, the Fed is safe.

Here's the irony: each side already holds the weapon that could crash the Fed — but they're too busy fighting each other to use it.

The **left's instinct** is to drain federal resources down into communities — to demand more benefits, more local programs, more redistribution. Every dollar siphoned from Washington into actual households weakens the central machine.

Crash The Fed

The **right's instinct** is to starve Washington by minimizing taxes — to keep resources out of the hands of the state. Every dollar not collected is a dollar the Fed cannot leverage into more debt.

Alone, each approach only blunts the system and creates division. Together, they're unstoppable. The Left can bleed the beast from one end while the Right cuts off its fuel from the other. If both sides understood that their instincts are not enemies but complements, the Fed would collapse under its own weight.

But as long as the divide keeps us distracted, that alliance never forms. So long as the debate remains left versus right, the Fed wins. The real choice is not between Democrats and Republicans. The real choice is between freedom and slavery, between honest money and perpetual theft.

The question is not: "Which party will save us?" The question is: "When will we stop falling for the trick, and when will we start using our shared leverage to crash the machine?"

To quote Super Soul from Vanishing Point, "The question is not when he's going to stop, but who is going to stop him."

> **Freedom is never voluntarily given by the oppressor; it must be demanded by the oppressed.**
> — Martin Luther King, Jr.

Lessons from History

We like to imagine that the crises of our time are new and unique. But history repeats itself because human nature is constant. Politicians seek power, bankers seek profit, and ordinary people are left to suffer the consequences, until they refuse to play along.

The fight against the Federal Reserve is not the first battle against financial tyranny. Every lesson from the past tells us the same thing: real change does not come from electing the right rulers. It comes from people acting outside the system.

The Civil Rights Movement is often remembered for speeches and marches, but its power came from economic action. When Black Americans in Montgomery refused to ride the buses for over a year, the city bled money. Laws were passed, and elections won — but only because the system was *forced* to change. Without economic hardship, the system would have had no real reason to bend to the will of a minority.

King understood a critical truth: **oppressors don't listen to ballots, they listen to lost revenue.** Especially oppressors who leverage corporations, lobbies and special interests to control politics.

The lesson for us is clear: the Fed will not be ended by voting harder. It will be ended when enough people refuse to fuel it — when we stop feeding the beast and start starving it of compliance.

In India, British rule was propped up not just by soldiers but by economic control. The British taxed salt — an essential commodity — and banned Indians from collecting their own. Gandhi's Salt March in 1930 was more than a protest. It was an act of defiance against the economic machinery of an empire.

By marching to the sea and making salt, ordinary people broke the law and broke the empire's monopoly. Britain's power collapsed not because Indians voted their way to freedom, but because they refused to obey unjust rules.

The Fed's legal tender monopoly is today's salt tax. It forces us to accept worthless paper in place of real value. The lesson from Gandhi is this: when people refuse to comply, the empire crumbles.

The fight against central banking is not new in America. President Andrew Jackson called the Second Bank of the United States a "den of vipers and thieves." He vetoed its recharter and paid off the national debt in 1835 — the only time in U.S. history it has been zero.

The bankers retaliated. Credit was contracted, panic ensued, and the economy collapsed in 1837. The establishment blamed Jackson, and the Bank's power eventually returned in a new form.

The lesson is sobering: even when a leader fights the system, it will fight back harder. Jackson's victory was temporary because it relied on a politician rather than a people's movement. Without mass resistance, the system regenerates.

When alcohol was banned in the 1920s, millions of Americans simply ignored the law. Speakeasies thrived, bootleggers became folk heroes, and the black market flourished. The government could not enforce its monopoly on morality because people refused to comply.

Prohibition ended not through voting, but through widespread civil disobedience that made the law unenforceable.

The Fed depends on a monopoly of money. But like alcohol under Prohibition, money is whatever people agree it is. If enough of us boycott FRNs and choose alternatives like gold, silver, Bitcoin, and barter, the Fed's monopoly becomes unenforceable too.

For decades, East Germans were told their system was permanent. The Berlin Wall stood as a symbol of tyranny. But in 1989, it collapsed not because a party voted it down, but because the people refused to comply. They marched, they defected, they tore at the wall with their own hands.

The most powerful regimes look invincible until they aren't. The Soviet bloc collapsed almost overnight when its citizens stopped believing in the lie.

The Fed's lie — that its paper is "money" — will end the same way. One day, enough people will refuse to accept it, and the wall of debt will crumble.

Perhaps the clearest lesson comes from America's own founding. The colonists did not win their freedom by sending delegates to London to negotiate. They boycotted British goods. They smuggled, they traded with silver and Spanish gold, they fought with their wallets long before they fought with muskets.

Tyranny was not voted away. It was starved, resisted, and finally defeated by people who withdrew consent.

In early 2022, thousands of truck drivers across Canada formed the Freedom Convoy, a rolling protest against government mandates that soon became a national shutdown. Within weeks, highways, border crossings, and supply routes were gridlocked. The capital city, Ottawa, was paralyzed. The government tried to ignore them—until the economy began to stall. Auto plants shut down for lack of parts, grocery shelves thinned, and billions in trade froze. In panic, Prime Minister Justin Trudeau invoked emergency powers that allowed banks to freeze protesters' accounts without due process. While this may sound like a loss for those involved, it revealed the truth that Trudeau was nothing more than a tyrant, wanting absolute control over his people, by brute force if necessary. This gained the truckers more support, and lost Trudeau some of his.

The episode proved two things: first, that ordinary workers still hold immense leverage when they withhold their labor; and second, that modern states will weaponize the financial system the moment citizens use economic pressure effectively. The truckers didn't need to storm Parliament. They just had to stop driving. Had they already freed themselves from state controlled banking, the government's retaliation would have had no effect.

Across Europe, farmers have been revolting against crippling taxes, fuel costs, and environmental mandates that threaten their survival. From the Netherlands to France, Germany, and Poland, tractors rolled into capital cities and blocked highways, ports, and distribution centers. In many of these countries, farmers dumped manure on government buildings and cut off supermarket supply lines to protest policies. The government threatened to seize their land in the name of "climate compliance." In France and Germany, convoys of tractors shut down city centers for days at a time, forcing governments to backtrack on new regulations.

These protests weren't riots—they were strategic economic blockades. By stopping the flow of food, fuel, and freight, farmers reminded the world that real power doesn't rest in parliaments or banks—it rests in the hands of those who keep the country fed.

Force is Their Last Resort

Every time in history that money began to lose its value, ordinary people did the same rational thing—they tried to protect themselves. In ancient Rome, as emperors shaved silver from the denarius and mixed it with cheaper metals, citizens quietly hoarded the older, heavier coins. Markets began to price the old and new money differently, exposing the government's deceit. Rome's response wasn't to restore honest coinage—it was to outlaw honesty. Anti-hoarding edicts and legal-tender decrees forced citizens to accept the debased coins at full value under threat of punishment.

The same pattern appeared in early America. As the Continental Congress printed "Continentals" into worthlessness, merchants and farmers refused to take them at face value. The government responded with legal-tender mandates and penalties for "refusing the people's money." It never worked. Prices soared, trade broke down, and the phrase "not worth a Continental" became a permanent warning etched into American memory.

These reactions have always betrayed fear. Tyrants know when their system is unraveling. When people start rejecting bad money, it's not just an economic act—it's an act of protest, a rejection of corruption itself. By outlawing that protest, governments reveal their weakness. They know their empire is rotting from within, and their only defense is to make the rot mandatory.

But in the end, the people always win. Empires collapse, currencies die, and governments fall—but life goes on. The people, their homes, their farms, their communities, their churches, their families, and their skills remain. The land still grows food. The black markets become the real markets. When tyrants lose control, it feels like catastrophe to them—but for everyone else, it is merely their first breath of freedom. The illusion falls apart, but the world does not.

The Pattern Is Clear

Every major shift in history shares the same pattern:
- **Oppressors never give up power willingly.**
- **Voting rarely produces fundamental change.**
- **Mass refusal, boycott, and disobedience do.**

The Fed is no different. Its monopoly is enforced not just by law but by our compliance. Break that compliance, and the system falls.

What these stories show is that freedom is not granted by rulers. It is seized by the people when they stop obeying.

The Fed will not be ended by electing the "right" president or passing a bill. It will be ended the same way empires, banks, and tyrannies have always fallen — when ordinary people decide enough is enough and act accordingly.

The Right must see that draining federal money into local communities is not just redistribution — it is weakening the empire. The Left must see that resisting taxation is not just selfishness — it is starving the beast that is starving the people. Together, these instincts can bring the system down faster than any vote ever could.

Part III
Crashing The Fed

I do not ask that you place hands upon the tyrant to topple him over, but simply that you support him no longer; then you will behold him, like a great Colossus whose pedestal has been pulled away, fall of his own weight and break in pieces.
— Étienne de La Boétie

Part III
Trashing the Fed

Understanding Markets

There are a few important concepts to understand about how markets behave. Some of these principles are often only really understood by market speculators and day traders, but they are an integral part of what will soon happen to Federal Reserve notes and Treasury bonds.

In an open market, those who have an asset list it for sale. The price they list it for is called the "ask," just like the "asking price." Similarly, those who want to buy the asset list their "bid," offering a price that they are willing to pay. At any given time, even when the asset is not trading, there may be many open orders. The open asks or sell orders will have higher prices, and the open bid or buy orders will have lower prices. If the prices overlap, the orders will be matched, completed and taken off the market. If nobody can agree on a price, there will be no sales.

This can be graphed on a chart called a "depth chart." This shows all the "open orders" or offers to buy or sell an asset. The height of the chart indicates how many shares of stock, bits of crypto, or grams of metals are in the open orders.

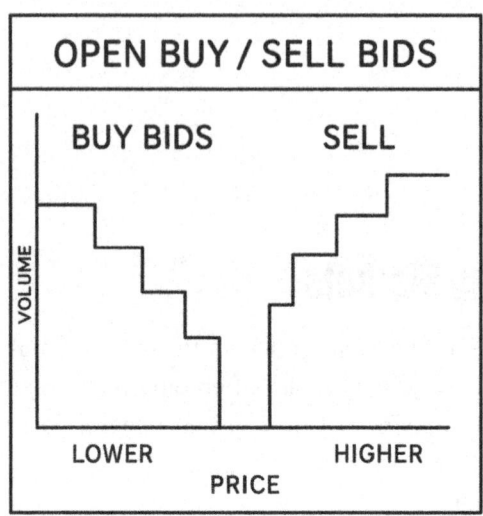

In this example chart, there are no matching orders, and the asset will not trade. A buyer, usually a "retail trader," can place a "market" order. If they want to buy 1,000 units, the market will match their order with whatever is for sale at whatever price. If the "ask" side of the depth chart starts at $5.00, but there are only 100 units for sale at that price, they will be matched. Whoever had the order open for 100 at $5 will get $500. But the retail buyer's order still has 900 units left to buy at the market price. If there are another 200 available for sale at $5.50, the market will match the order. This seller will receive $1,100 and the buyer will receive the 200 shares. This will continue until all 1,000 units have been matched.

The exact same thing happens if you have 1,000 units of the asset to sell. You'll first match with the highest bid, then the next highest bid, then the next, progressively reducing the price at which you are selling this asset.

You can imagine how, if someone placed a massive market order, the price could quickly get out of hand. If you have a lot to sell, the price could quickly drop. This is why there are so many open orders on the depth chart that just aren't trading. If someone has a million shares to sell, placing an open market order could quickly exhaust all the bids. There very well may be some sharks sitting with open orders for very low prices. They do this knowing that an asset may be worth more, but if someone needs to get rid of their stake, they can capitalize on a cheap price. Since all the other bids would have been taken, they can't turn around and drop it back on the market, but they might wait for a little bit for some more of those orders to start showing up, then slowly sell them back at a higher price.

Most people talk about the price of these assets, but there isn't really a price on the market. The price is determined by the entire set of open orders. When we see a price on a ticker or a quote on a stock chart, we'll sometimes see it noted as the "last" price. Whether it says that or not, what you are really looking at is simply the price at which the last trade was made. That does not mean that if you place an order for that price that it will be matched, especially if you are looking to buy a very large number of that asset. You may sometimes see the bid and ask prices printed, which are actual offers.

There are many reasons someone might want to get rid of their assets quickly, like if they have leveraged their stake. If the price falls below a certain threshold, the market might force them to sell their shares at market price, just to make sure they are sold before they fall any lower. They might also need cash for some other reason, like to invest in another opportunity. They might be willing to take a loss, but they need cash quickly.

Imagine a bank has a million ounces of gold. They need cash because a lot of customers have been withdrawing funds. If they don't have any cash on hand, the feds will say they are insolvent and shut them down. So they do what they have to, and dump 1 million ounces of gold on the open market. Depending on their circumstances, they may do this gradually to keep the price of gold from plummeting. Regardless how much, the price will fall. They are not putting it on the market with an asking price, because they need the cash. They are picking up any bid they can find. They are also looking at averages. If there are more higher bids, they can take other bids that are even lower, because the average is still higher. But the lowest bids always come last, and this is what people see as the market price. The gap on the depth chart is wider, because in this short amount of time, no new bids or asks have come in.

This is why we often see news articles reporting on billionaires or large institutions that are buying or selling large amounts of a certain asset. Savvy investors see this and know how it can affect the markets and influence other investors.

Some traders may open new orders to buy at even lower prices, speculating that the bank might have more to get rid of soon. Others with open sell orders at higher prices might lose confidence and lower their asks, hoping that it brings the price back up. Then there are those who will see the price fall, panic, and decide it's a good time to get out. This results in panic selling, where some large investors or many small investors, simultaneously open orders to sell. This drags the price down further and the cycle continues. Eventually it stops, because there are still a lot of people that will hold onto these assets forever, knowing that they will always hold value.

Promises behave the same way in these markets, but unlike the assets mentioned so far, promises can be broken.

If a company is not doing well, shareholders might dump the stock until single shares are trading for fractions of a penny. These companies are obligated to be transparent with their finances. If a company is truly worthless, everyone will know and will try to get rid of their shares. But you can't sell your shares if nobody is buying, and who would want to buy such a stock? There may be day traders hoping to capitalize on small price swings, or other speculators who buy this company cheap as a gamble. Some others might try to buy up all the stock hoping to win when the company's assets are liquidated. But all of these people are looking to buy at the lowest price possible, and most people are willing to sell it for whatever they can get.

These circumstances bring up another important dynamic called liquidity, usually measured in volume. If nobody wants to trade an asset, you can place market orders all day, and it will never get filled. The volume has dropped to zero, and there are no offers at all. There can be offers to buy or sell, but with a wide gap between them, and no market orders. If the asset is said to be illiquid, it means you either can't buy it or can't sell it. Typically, it means you can't sell it. If the asset is liquid, that means there are a lot of people actively trading it, and you should have no problem buying or selling, relatively close to the market price.

As assets lose their value, the price can drop to almost nothing, followed by a period where nobody wants to buy it at all. It's garbage that nobody wants to pick up, even if it's free. It's avoided like the plague. If you're holding this asset, you won't be able to sell it for any price, or even give it away. Imagine if this happened with your dollars.

Government bonds are not backed by government assets, precious metals, cryptocurrencies, or anything else. They are simply promises backed by more promises. If the dollar begins to fail, people will want to get rid of their dollars as fast as possible. This means that they will be dumping those dollars into any market they can find, to buy anything that will hold its value longer. That includes stocks, metals, cryptocurrencies, foreign currencies, or anything else.

These all have markets with bids and asks. When people and institutions dump billions of FRNs, you will see a massive number of market bids. Prices will skyrocket because all the open asks will be taken at whatever they are. Those who are savvy will even see this trend, take their current asks off the market and put them back on with even higher asks.

Government bonds are traded the same way, although they are derivative. Anyone holding these bonds will be just as eager to get rid of them. If holding FRNs is like holding stock for a failing company, then holding Treasury bonds is like holding shares in a mutual fund that holds shares in the failing company.

Though people don't like paying high prices for these assets, they will want to get rid of these FRNs before they become illiquid. At that point, they won't be able to get anything for them.

It's important to understand that these are not markets to buy and sell assets. They are markets to trade one asset for another. They are two-sided, and they work the same way in either direction. In fact, there are markets where you can trade one cryptocurrency for another directly, or cryptocurrencies for precious metals. If you think of your money in terms of gold, then you might prefer to look at a mirror image of the depth chart used by someone who thinks of FRNs as money. That is, they will think they are buying and selling gold for FRNs while you think you are buying and selling FRNs for gold. In the same way, when the price of gold in dollars is going up for them, the price of dollars in gold is going down for you.

If you were to look at the price of dollars in the amount of gold it costs to buy them, you would see that it's been declining constantly since the Fed was created. The more people want to get rid of them, the fewer bids there will be, and the prices will only get lower. At some point, just like every other failed currency, it will become illiquid. You won't be able to trade any of your FRNs for any other asset.

Doesn't this make you want to sell those dollars even more quickly?

This works in the real world also. When you walk into a store, products are placed on the shelf with an "ask" price. Knowing that this is the market price, you may or may not decide to buy. The higher the price, the less likely you will agree to it. The lower the price, the supply will be quickly matched with buyers. This is how you get shortages when governments force prices down. It's how you get economic control over businesses by boycotting, effectively making their business illiquid.

Though these markets look completely different from trading markets, they function the same way. Someone has a product or a service, and someone else has FRNs. Some people are willing to spend one amount and other people are willing to ask for another amount. Trade happens when they meet in the middle, and any asset can become illiquid if nobody wants it.

The government, like a failing, publicly traded company, has to publish their financial statements. We know that the government's debt is growing uncontrollably. We know that money is simply their promise. We know that they will routinely break their promises, refusing to give us anything in exchange for our FRNs. As the debt increases, more money will be printed. Inflation will continue, and those trying to minimize their exposure will dump their dollars and their derivatives. This money will flow into all of the many markets that trade in dollars. The inflow of cash will exhaust all the open ask orders, causing more people to list their assets for sale at even higher prices.

Eventually, with no end in sight for the falling price of the dollar, people will stop listing their assets for sale in FRNs. They might switch to other markets where they can list their assets to exchange for other assets like cryptocurrencies. The dollar will become illiquid, first in one market, then another, until few markets are trading in dollars at all.

As fewer people have any use for the dollar, the government will have a hard time using them to pay their contractors and employees. They will be forced to print them faster. Nobody will accept their worthless bonds, as their interest rates would have to be higher than the rate of inflation. A 10% bond with 100% inflation is worthless. A 1,000% bond with 100% inflation today, would only force the rate of inflation up above 1,000% when people try to cash in those bonds. Few people will bother to buy these unless they are being scammed or trying to scam someone else.

The combination of faster printing and refusal to accept dollars will compound, accelerating the dollar into a downward spiral. Eventually you won't be able to buy anything with it at all. I could predict that they would be found littering the streets, but the truth is that most of this will happen digitally. Instead, we're more likely to see bank accounts with balances of billions of dollars, abandoned, as they are completely worthless.

The government will try to force people to accept these notes, but history has proven they can only do that for a short time before it all falls apart.

The Real-World Consequences

When Ron Paul says "End the Fed" or I say "Crash the Fed," someone inevitably asks: *"But what happens next?"* It's an important question. We are so entangled with the Federal Reserve system that its collapse sounds unthinkable.

And yet history teaches us that no fiat currency lasts forever. Collapse is not a possibility; it is a certainty. The only uncertainty is timing and the form it takes. So the real question isn't whether the Fed will fall — but what that fall means for ordinary Americans.

The dollar feels stable only because it has been the standard for over a century. You're paid in dollars, you save in dollars, you shop in dollars, and you pay taxes in dollars. It feels permanent because we've never known anything else.

But stability is an illusion. Since 1913, the dollar has lost over 99% of its purchasing power. What you could buy for a dollar then now costs over $25. Wages, pensions, savings accounts — all eroded slowly enough that people mistake theft for "progress."

A collapse would simply make the theft obvious all at once.

From time to time, inflation's effects play out in such a way that everyone notices a steep surge in prices or their products getting smaller through shrinkflation. This is attributed to anything from greedy corporations to incompetent politicians. Few consider that this is an inevitable effect of using a single currency as a measure of value that is based upon the printing habits of a single bank. This is like trying to measure the size of an object with an elastic ruler.

But while inflation shows a slow deterioration of value, eliminating the dollar would completely obliterate it. A power vacuum would form, destroying everything that depends on the dollar, creating space for new currencies and systems to enter the market.

The Collapse Scenario

When the Fed's system finally breaks, here's what you can expect:

1. **Treasury Bonds Become Worthless:**
   Many call U.S. Treasuries the "safest asset in the world." That's a lie sustained only by faith. If the dollar collapses, who wants a piece of paper promising repayment in more dollars? The supposed bedrock of the global financial system will turn into confetti.
2. **Retirement Accounts:**
   Trillions of dollars sit in pensions, 401(k)s, IRAs — often invested in dollar assets like Treasury bonds. While treasury bonds will become worthless, other investments like stocks are likely to remain valuable. Stocks are valued in dollars, but they are not backed by dollars. They are dependent on a company's ability to survive troubled times. Many companies on the market today have been around since before the great depression, and others formed more recently have survived other market crashes since. Some companies provide products that will always be needed and also hold real assets like land, mines, and factories. Even under hyperinflation, these companies are valuable.
3. **Hyperinflation or Default:**
   The government will face a choice: print to cover obligations, causing hyperinflation, or default on debt and obligations, causing a financial freeze. Either way, the result is pain: your dollars lose value or the money pipeline shuts off.
4. **Supply Chains Break:**
   America imports vast amounts of goods — food, fuel, medicine, electronics. If foreign nations stop accepting dollars, shelves go empty. Gas stations ration fuel. Pharmacies run out of prescriptions.

It won't be theoretical; it will be felt in every household. This is only temporary, of course. Most countries know that they used to hold dollars because they could be redeemed for gold. They were stabbed in the back by Nixon, and many still hold a grudge. They know gold is more valuable, and many countries are also looking to Bitcoin as an alternative for storing value and international trade.

5. **Bank Runs and Frozen Accounts:**
In a crisis, people rush to withdraw. Banks close doors. ATMs limit cash. Politicians declare "bank holidays." Your money is no longer yours. It's locked until the crisis passes. These days, it's more likely that the Fed will just print its unlimited supply of cash to keep the ATMs running, but that will only accelerate inflation. ATMs will only be empty for the time it takes delivery trucks to refill them.

The Political Fallout: Tricks to Expect

Crises are opportunities for the state. When people are scared, they accept controls they would normally resist, especially when politicians bundle them up in bills with fun and positive sounding names. In a collapse, we should expect the government to point blame at bad actors, claiming themselves, their bureaucracies and their Federal Reserve system to be benevolent. They will impose new laws to try to prevent the collapse of their system. They will exaggerate the effects of the crisis, and even add to it by instigating conflicts and threatening to shut down the government. They know that the bigger the problem appears, the more power they have to manufacture support for themselves to act as saviors.

We may see programs like:
- **Capital Controls.** Restrictions on moving money abroad. Prohibitions on cryptocurrencies. Stricter legal tender laws and enforcement. Regulations on gold and silver. Limits on converting to gold or crypto. They will blame criminals, as always. Anti-money laundering laws (AML) and Know Your Customer requirements (KYC) will claim they are stopping international drug smugglers and money launderers. In reality, it only makes it harder for companies to provide transactional services to ordinary people. Similarly, when

Nixon stopped returning gold to the countries which trusted the U.S. to hold it, he blamed money speculators, when it was their own mismanagement that left them unable to fulfill their promises.
- **Price Controls.** Politicians will try to outlaw "gouging." The result will be empty shelves.
- **Rationing.** Fuel, food, and medicine distributed by political favor. Friends of the regime eat first. Regulations can give government control of access to anything for sale, even if the government isn't the one actually distributing it. Control of transportation through highway inspections, border checkpoints, and other choke points can give them full control over resource distribution.
- **Emergency Powers.** Congress and the president will declare "temporary measures" that never end. Surveillance, restrictions, asset seizures — all justified by "stability."
- **A "New Fed."** When the dust settles, they'll propose a replacement: a Central Bank Digital Currency (CBDC). Marketed as a fix, it will be Fed 2.0 — programmable money with total surveillance and no escape hatch.

The trick is always the same: use the crisis to grab more power.

In order to prevent their tricks from working, those involved can't just be involved because it's fashionable or popular. It is imperative that those involved understand what we are fighting for. It's not just to End the Fed, it's to get government out of our finances, and regain our economic power.

Not the End of the World

All of this sounds dire — and it is. But collapse is not the end of the world. It is the end of *their* world.

People adapt. Communities rebuild. Trade finds a way. Collapse clears out the rot. The parasites who lived off the debt machine lose their power. The slate is wiped clean for something new.

Those who suffer the most will be those more dependent on the system. Government workers whose pensions vanish. Citizens with wealth in dollar backed securities will lose their wealth. But they have an opportunity now to rearrange their finances. This isn't the end of the world.

Those hit hardest who don't deserve it will be those living on fixed government incomes, but the prosperity that follows will allow more community action to replace the government safety net. More people will be lifted out of poverty in the following months and years.

Many will thrive in the collapse, like those who have already become independent from government systems. People holding real assets like land, metals, skills, food stores will live as if nothing happened. Communities with parallel systems of trade and trust will be sheltered from the fallout of the collapsing dollar. Anyone prepared to transact outside the Fed's monopoly, with a store of precious metals, cryptocurrencies and other valuable assets, will have a solid foundation for trade. And as they trade, those assets will circulate into new communities, bringing that wealth back to those who were unprepared for the collapse.

The crash is not the end. It's a new beginning. It is a transfer of power from those who rely on the system to those who reject it.

The Necessary Pain

It is tempting to ask: can't we avoid collapse by reforming the system? The answer is no. The system itself is the problem. The debt machine cannot be tamed. The Fed cannot be reformed into honesty. Collapse is the cure — painful, but necessary.

Like a drug addict hitting rock bottom, the nation cannot heal until the system breaks.

Knowing what collapse looks like is the first step in preparing for it. That means:
- Diversifying into real assets.
- Building community ties.
- Learning self-sufficiency skills.
- Developing trust networks outside the dollar system.

The crash will hurt only for those caught unprepared. For those ready, it is survivable — even liberating.

The real-world consequences of crashing the Fed are not academic. They are personal. They will be measured in empty shelves, broken pensions, and panicked neighbors. But they will also be measured in new opportunities, stronger communities, and the rebirth of freedom.

Every empire that debased its currency has fallen. The Fed's empire will fall too. The only question is whether you will fall with it, or prosper with those who stand aside and let it fall.

Preparing For the Crash

When people first hear about the inevitable collapse of the Fed's system, they react with fear. That's natural. If your entire life has been denominated in dollars, the thought of those dollars vanishing is terrifying.

But fear is not the right response. Preparation is. Collapse is not the end of the world — it is the end of *their* world. Those who prepare will not only survive; many will thrive. The key is to act before the crash, not during it.

Remember, many people made fortunes during the great depression by simply buying cheap stock in a crashed market.

Step 1: Get Out of the Paper Trap

The first rule is simple: **don't be the last one holding the hot potato.** The Fed's paper will eventually become worthless. The goal is to trade it for real value while you still can.

Think of anything tied to dollars as a hot potato. You can hold it for a little while, but you don't want to be the one still clutching it when the music stops.

- **Cash:** Keep some for emergencies and short-term needs, but don't hoard large amounts. Inflation erodes it daily, and in a collapse it will buy less each week. Keeping millions in your mattress is not a smart strategy.
- **Treasury Bonds:** Avoid them at all costs. Holding Treasuries, whether directly or inside your 401(k), is literally investing in and

betting on the dollar and the Fed. When the Fed ends, they will be worthless scraps of paper.
- **401(k)s and Pensions:** Many of these are built on government debt and dollar-backed promises. Even though the Fed and the federal government are technically separate, the government's obligations are only as good as Federal Reserve Notes. If the dollar collapses, so do the promises. If your 401(k) doesn't let you get away from treasury notes, there are ways to roll your savings over into other retirement accounts with better options, and without paying the tax penalty, like IRAs.
- **Stocks:** Equities in real businesses are not as bad — companies can survive even if the dollar doesn't. But stock markets are denominated in dollars, so values will still swing wildly in a collapse. Stocks can be a piece of your plan, but don't put all your eggs in one basket. Many companies that are not prepared will go under. There is always great opportunity in crashing markets. Hyperinflation means more money, which means higher stock prices. If they fall, that means people are getting their money out of the market. It means they are selling at panic prices. This can be an excellent opportunity to buy cheap stock in companies that will likely survive the collapse. This strategy has historically made some people very wealthy.

Promises can be broken. Every dollar you shift out of paper promises and into something real is a step toward survival.

Step 2: Acquire Real Assets

Real wealth is not numbers on a screen. It is the things with intrinsic or lasting value.
- **Gold and Silver.** For thousands of years, these have been money. They cannot be printed, and they hold value through every collapse. While collecting gold and silver has been recently limited to connoisseurs and preppers, more people will see the value of these metals when they are faced with a complete devaluation of fiat. Even if you don't know a whole lot of people who value gold as money, every government around the world does.

- **Bitcoin and Crypto.** Digital assets allow for borderless trade and censorship resistance. Not all coins are equal — Bitcoin and privacy-focused coins like Monero matter most. Others are popular like Ethereum, Solana, and Doge. There are thousands of coins out there, but the most important thing aside from the properties and policies of the coin itself is adoption. There isn't much use for a coin that nobody accepts, and pump and dump scams with new tokens are all over the place. Everyone has their own opinion on which coin is best, just don't fall for the scams. Stick with time tested coins that already have a large user base. DeFi or decentralized finance ensures that even if someone prefers different coins than you, transactions can still be made, converting the currency nearly instantaneously.
- **Land.** Soil that grows food is worth more than paper that buys it. Land also provides security, independence, and bargaining power. The further away from major cities, the better. Within city limits you have more governments competing to take what you have. Outside city limits, things are too decentralized for feds to go door to door, kicking everyone off their property. You have far more freedom to produce your own food and energy.
- **Food, Water, and Power.** I lose a lot of people here because few want to farm their own food, collect rain water or build solar arrays. It's convenient just to have that provided, even at some cost. But just as with everything else, the more you depend on someone else, the more you will be impacted by fluctuations in the economy. Even if you don't want to do the work yourself, support your neighbors against regulations that prohibit solar or wind energy, grid disconnection, water collection, or livestock. Those noisy chickens that your neighbors have might soon feed you.
- **Tools and Skills.** A well-stocked workshop or a skill in demand can be more valuable than gold. The neighbors in your community who have put in all the work to build distributed systems will be happy to help you if you're happy to help them. Anyone can learn skills, as long as you have a desire to learn. Most people lack these skills simply for the fact that they don't believe they are necessary and have no desire to learn them.

- **Medicine and First Aid.** Learn some of the basics. Many people have become far too accustomed to a doctor's visit for small problems. You don't need to become a doctor, but knowing some basic first aid and having some common medicines and supplies on hand will mean less dependence on a healthcare system with prices and accessibility unknown.

Preparation means trading in that fragile paper for durable value.

I want to emphasize that I don't expect power grids and food supplies to break down completely. I do expect interruptions and high prices. The more people who can break away from that system, the fewer people will be affected. That also means that panic buyers have less effect on the markets. Your independence helps others survive turbulent times by being one less mouth for the centralized system to feed.

I also want to emphasize that for these same reasons, we should all work for this kind of independence – collapse or not. It can sometimes be difficult to accept change in our lives, but the more independent you become from these systems, the more you realize you were overdependent on them. Ultimately we make our own decisions, and many of us make choices that result in others taking advantage of us.

Step 3: Strengthen Your Community

The lone-wolf survivalist is a Hollywood fantasy. In reality, collapse favors communities. Mutual aid, trust networks, and local cooperation are the real safety nets. Get to know your neighbors. Learn from them. Teach them. Work on projects together. Help them with one of their projects in exchange for them helping you with one of yours.

There are too many benefits to name them all. Knowing your neighbors, whether in an apartment building or a rural setting, is extremely important. Imagine someone is attacking you in front of your home, but you've never even met your neighbors. They happen to pass by and see the fight. Will they want to step in and help? Will they even know who the good guy is?

You don't have to start a cult or sign contracts with your neighbors for protection. Just getting to know them creates a bond that encourages people to look out for each other. It gives them information they need to know whether someone is entering the place they live or breaking in. Be kind to them. That doesn't mean let them take advantage of you. You should set your boundaries. But don't disrespect them or their boundaries. Be friendly. Let them know you have their back.

When the Fed collapses, the strongest currency will be trust.

Step 4: Minimize Your Exposure to the State

The government will not go quietly. When the system cracks, expect new taxes, seizures, and controls. Preparation means minimizing your vulnerability.

- **Legal Tax Minimization.** Use every deduction, loophole, and structure available. The less you feed the beast, the less it can spend.
- **Avoid Debt Dependence.** Mortgages, car loans, credit cards — these keep you chained to the system and could go either way. With hyperinflation, your predetermined loan payments could drop to the cost of a cup of coffee, but high prices might mean that you don't have any income, miss payments, and the bank takes everything. That doesn't mean to not take on debt at all. Debt can be leveraged to buy harder assets that will retain value beyond the crash, with loans that will be easy to pay back with devalued dollars. But don't over extend yourself with collateralized loans that make you vulnerable to repossession.
- **Own Things Directly.** If you don't hold it, you don't own it. Paper claims are the first to vanish. In 2021, the FBI raided and seized assets from an entire safety deposit vault of 700 to 800 boxes. In 2022, Peter Schiff's bank in Puerto Rico was seized. As of the publication of this book, all of his customers have yet to have access to their funds, even though the bank was completely solvent.

The less the state can take from you, the freer you are to survive the collapse. Centralization makes it easy for them. Regulated banks keep everything on record and comply with regulations. That means the government knows where they are at all times. They have a catalog of entities to read through and decide to seize. A simple letter can empty out many accounts at once. They can take the assets of millions of people all in one fell swoop. With distributed possession, it's far more complicated, and takes a lot more man power to collect from that many people. The more difficult their job, the fewer people they can reach, and the less disastrous the impact of the crash.

Step 5: Psychological Readiness

Collapse isn't just material. It is mental. When neighbors panic, when headlines scream, when politicians promise salvation through new controls — the prepared must stay calm.

- **Expect volatility.** Prices will swing, rumors will spread, fear will dominate. Don't let it dictate your actions. Recognize all of that for what it is. The politicians through the media are trying to convince you to give them control to fix the problem. The problem only exists because they abused their power. Don't give it back to them. They are only looking to regain power.
- **See through the propaganda.** Every crisis will be blamed on "greedy corporations," "hoarders," or "foreign enemies." They may even accuse anyone holding the book you're reading right now as being a domestic terrorist. This is something they have already done in the past, with the FBI declaring groups like libertarians to be terrorist organizations.
- **Stay principled.** Collapse tests morality. Theft, betrayal, violence will tempt many. Refuse to become what you fight against. Distance yourself from instigators and avoid getting into other people's fights. Share the strategy of this book with as many people as will listen, but if they show strong emotional opposition, don't push too hard. Sometimes those who seem too far gone just need a couple seeds planted and they will come around when the time is right. Pushing them too hard all at once will only create enemies and resistance.

The Opportunity in Collapse

It is easy to see collapse as a loss. But for those prepared, it is an opportunity. The opportunity to build stronger, freer communities. The opportunity to exchange directly, without government regulation or intervention, and with the freedom to choose any currency to transact. The opportunity to finally throw off the chains of the debt machine.

Every collapse in history has created winners and losers. The losers were those who trusted the system. The winners were those who prepared before it broke.

The time to prepare is not after the headlines announce panic. It is now. Every dollar you move into real assets, every jar you put on a shelf, every neighbor you build trust with is insurance against the inevitable.

The Fed's collapse will not be gentle. But it will be survivable. And for those ready, it will be liberating.

You can't stop the storm. But you can build a house that weathers it.

What Happens to the Dollar

For over a century, the dollar has been treated as if it were eternal. The world calls it the "reserve currency," nations stockpile it in vaults, and Americans assume it will always be the unit of value.

But history mocks the idea of permanence. Every fiat currency that has ever existed has collapsed. Rome's denarius, France's assignats, Germany's papiermarks, Zimbabwe's trillion-dollar notes, and Venezuela's million percent inflation — all followed the same path: debasement, inflation, collapse.

The question is not *if* the dollar dies. The question is *how and when*.

The most familiar path is inflation — the gradual erosion of purchasing power. It is already happening. Since the Fed's creation in 1913, the dollar has lost 97% of its value. A gallon of gas that cost 5 cents then costs over $4 today.

For most people, inflation is invisible theft. Wages rise in nominal terms, but purchasing power stagnates or falls. Savers see their nest eggs eaten away. It feels "normal" because it is slow. But slow death is still death.

If the Fed continues on its current trajectory, the dollar may limp along for years, each decade hollowing out more of its value until people finally abandon it.

Inflation inevitably leads to hyperinflation. When a currency inflates, the cost of the government's expenses also rises. Sometimes this is delayed, but the faster they print, the faster government contractors realize they can increase their bids. The government can either raise taxes on people whom the new money hasn't filtered down to yet, or it can just print more. Eventually this spirals out of control.

While inflation is often blamed on printing money, there are other contributors. Printing money does inflate the money supply, but so does fractional reserve lending. The lower the reserve rate, the more infinite the pool of money fabricated from lending. In recent years, that reserve rate has been lowered to 0%. This further exacerbates the higher prices in all markets, as more money is available for anything.

Something else to consider is that market prices are the result of supply and demand. If people no longer demand fiat, they'll want to get rid of it as soon as possible. This leads to an increased supply of money – not in standard terms where the money supply increases, but in terms of how much of that money is in the market, chasing something else. Imagine what would happen when people with lots of liquid fiat are trying to get rid of it. What do they do? They might buy stocks, metals or cryptos, or stockpile food. All of this money flooding into those markets raises those prices.

As prices climb, people realize that holding onto this currency is a losing strategy. More and more people will wake up to this and join in, accelerating the climbing prices.

But this isn't what's happening. Prices of goods aren't going up. The value of the dollar is going down. Something that nobody wants has little value. We think of buying and selling things in terms of dollars because that's the world we grew up in. But people aren't buying everything they can – they are getting rid of the dollars before they become worthless. The media and politicians will treat this just like any other inflation. They'll blame greedy corporations. They'll say markets are in a bubble. They'll point at scapegoats and make up any story they can, but they'll never tell the truth: the dollar is failing.

Could it happen in the U.S.? Yes. The trillions printed in 2008 and 2020 were the opening moves. Once foreign confidence breaks, hyperinflation is the logical endgame.

The dollar's power is not just domestic. It is global. Since World War II, oil and trade have been priced in dollars. Foreign nations hold trillions in U.S. debt. This "exorbitant privilege" allows America to import goods by exporting paper.

But what happens when the world stops playing along? Already, the BRICS nations (Brazil, Russia, India, China, and Saudi Arabia started the growing list) are building systems to bypass the dollar in oil trade. Central banks worldwide are stockpiling gold at the fastest pace in decades.

The moment foreign confidence breaks, the flood of dollars abroad will come rushing home, and be refused as payment for exports to the U.S. Those dollars will compete with domestic supply, triggering inflation or hyperinflation overnight. The dollar's global empire will implode, and Americans will feel the cost directly at the gas pump and grocery store.

When fiat currencies collapse, governments rarely admit defeat. Instead, they announce a "reset." Old notes are swapped for new ones. Zeros are removed. A "temporary emergency measure" becomes the new standard.

Expect the same here. When the dollar breaks, Washington and the Fed will roll out a "New Dollar." Most likely, it will be digital — a Central Bank Digital Currency (CBDC). Marketed as stability, it will be programmable money: every transaction tracked, every dollar controlled. Expiration dates, spending restrictions, instant tax collection — the dream of every tyrant.

While many conspiracy theorists claim that this will be the only money, I don't see that happening. I do believe that there will still be some sort of coinage or paper that can be converted. The reason for this is that while the government wants to track all of our transactions, this would create too many problems. Those in areas with sparse connectivity will complain that they can't transact without the internet or power. There are also plenty of insiders in government positions who benefit from the cover of secrecy available in cash transactions.

While I don't believe cash will be eliminated, I do believe the push to use their digital currency will make it difficult to do business in many ways with alternate currencies. Most people will have a hard time circumventing the system and be stuck struggling to work within the confines of regulation.

With this comes good and bad. People will lose trust in the government's dollar, and it will be hard for the government to recover. People will not be easily swayed to accept a new currency that comes from the same people who produced the last, greatly flawed currency. Debts like mortgages could be washed away or settled for far less than what is owed. That's good for you but bad for the banks. It could also be bad for you if people owe you money, or if you have fixed contracts. You might need to renegotiate those in a more stable currency. Doing this ahead of time is smarter.

It's important to remember that hard assets are hard assets. People too often look at the value of things in dollars. If you own a home and the land it sits on, that is a home and land. That never changes. You can look on Zillow and watch the prices go up and down, but those are only speculative. If the currency swings one way or another, your house is still a house. It's still going to provide you shelter. The land can still provide food. Don't let market prices fool you into thinking you should sell your hard assets "before it's too late."

The dollar's end will be messy, painful, and unavoidable. The exact form may differ — slow inflation, hyperinflation, deflation, rejection, or reset — but the result is the same: the end of trust in paper promises.

For those unprepared, it will be devastating. For those ready, it will be liberating. When the old paper dies, the chance to build something new is born.

The dollar is not permanent. It never was.

Avoiding a Fed 2.0

Thomas Sowell was asked about Ron Paul's position on ending the Fed. He was asked if the Fed were removed, what would it be replaced with? Sowell replied, "When someone removes a cancer what do you replace it with?"

While this is a great answer, affirming that there is no need for the Federal Reserve, it doesn't really answer the question. The question is deeper than this. If you're asking how the government will print or borrow money, then sure, it's a great answer. But if you're asking what money we will use, it's not a very good answer at all.

Many have already jumped in to say that gold, silver, and cryptocurrencies will replace it. That's great, but what does that transition look like?

Can we just eliminate the Fed and assume everything will be sunshine and rainbows from that day forward? What about the trillions of Federal Reserve notes that are still circulating? What about the treasury notes and bonds in Average Joe's retirement account? Do we just burn it all? How will the economy work? Will everyone have to barter or will we use other money? Will there be a transitional period or policy?

When someone says they don't want to replace the Fed with anything, they mean in place of a central bank. While this is great, there are other voids that need to be filled, and will be filled. Being prepared to answer this ahead of time will help to make a more peaceful transition.

Not knowing the answer means the same people who benefit from the Fed will set up to fill it with something just as bad. It sets us up to be led by untrustworthy politicians right back to the very same place.

Many advocate a new gold backed currency, but that's just as bad as what we have now — and for the same reason. A single currency will be controlled by a single governing body. Even if it starts out with benevolent intent, it's a ripe target for the corrupt. Remember that it only took one executive order in 1933 to outlaw private gold ownership, and one executive order in 1971 to declare gold notes as unredeemable. That happened under the same system of elected officials, courts, separate branches, bicameral legislation, and all the other checks and balances we have today. If this were done outside of the government, there would be even less public scrutiny. It's only a matter of time until someone with bad intentions worms their way into controlling the printing press – public or private.

Good times can't last forever, no matter what kind of checks and balances you can imagine. It is centralized, and centralization is flawed.

A decentralized model would be better, but there are still a lot of problems to solve. Who gets to issue the notes, how do you know which notes are real, and which issuers can be trusted to have the gold to be redeemed? Who will audit them?

Cryptocurrencies have many advantages over a gold backed system, but create a host of other problems, especially for those who don't understand the technology or the importance of securing their own private keys and wallets.

These are all difficult problems to solve, and should be solved ahead of time. As a single person, I can only put forth my opinion on what I would like to see, but that should never bar others from using what they prefer. How do we interface with each other and prevent isolated markets that can't trade because they don't use the same systems?

The best solution to any complex problem is chaos. Chaos has been given a bad name, but it's commonly misunderstood. Chaos is often blamed for problems by politicians who want to implement their central controls, but is simply the result of individuals acting in the way that serves them best, with the freedom to decide their own destiny. Chaos is not violence. It's disorder. It's simply the absence of everyone doing the same thing, usually by force. When chaos is embraced, rather than feared, it will produce superior outcomes to any central planning.

The market may be flooded with hot new ideas, many which collapse after just a few months or years. But giving people the freedom to test different currencies and decide what works best for them will result in the selection of the best money for society. It won't just be one winner and it doesn't need to be locked in forever. There will likely be more than one winner that creates the opportunity for new technologies or services to allow people using different currencies to connect, the way credit card companies seamlessly allow you to spend your USD when you're traveling abroad.

This is possibly one of the most important points of this book. It is easy to be guided by our own desires. Even the most fervent freedom activists have their own strong beliefs about certain things. I want to say "unless you are an absolute anarchist", but even anarchists have opinions on what should and shouldn't exist in this world. More freedom enthusiasts than you think would be quick to support a law making one type of money the one that runs the entire economy. It's not coming from an authoritarian intention, so much as a belief that one currency would make everything better, and supporting their favorite. We have to understand that this is wrong, even if it makes answering some other questions above easier.

Central planning and consolidation is how we got here in the first place. We don't have to pick a single monetary system. It's better if we don't. As the chaos theorist, Dr. Ian Malcolm said in Jurassic Park, "life finds a way."

Many people assume that once the Federal Reserve is gone, the problem is solved. But that assumption is dangerous. If we're not careful, the Fed's collapse will simply become the excuse for its replacement — a "Fed 2.0" that makes the original look tame.

The establishment will not give up control of money willingly. If their current racket collapses, they will immediately try to build a new one. And history shows that when governments are handed a crisis, they use it to seize more power, not less. If we are not prepared, they will be, and we'll end up with a Fed 2.0.

Transitioning

Part of keeping ourselves out of the Fed 2.0 trap is understanding the transition. Ending the Fed is only the first half of the fight. The real battle will be in the aftermath, when politicians try to slip in Fed 2.0 as the "solution."

If people fall for it, nothing changes — except the chains get tighter. But if people see through it, if they refuse to accept the replacement, then the crash becomes liberation instead of substitution.

This means we have to know what to expect and how to behave. The further in advance problems are solved, the smoother the transition will be.

There are hundreds of millions of Americans. A vast majority of them have lived their entire life knowing only one currency. They believe it will last forever. They don't understand the monetary system, and would resist using anything else.

If you've ever traveled abroad, you know that when you first enter a new economy where everything is priced in a different currency, you're constantly trying to convert those prices back into dollars. That's because the money you have was earned in dollars. Imagine trying to convert these prices into meaningful ounces of silver or Satoshis of Bitcoin.

This doesn't work, because subconsciously we're trying to find something to relate the prices to. If everything we know is in dollars, we relate it to that. We know how much we expect to pay for a regular meal, a fast cheap meal, or a fancy expensive meal. If prices are too high we say it's expensive. If they are too low, we call them cheap. But that's because we have trained our brain in one currency for most of our lives.

This extends to things you have never done before. If you went to a new amusement park, the ticket price may or may not shock you. You have no frame of reference to what that park usually costs. You don't know if their prices have recently increased. But your brain is subconsciously comparing this to many other things that you do know. How does the price of admission compare to a fancy meal, a night in a hotel, a car payment, mortgage payment or rent payment? Everything is in the same currency so it's easy to compare.

Things are skewed during inflation, but this also impacts our ability to determine whether prices are too high or low. Imagine, kids today think the normal price of a cup of coffee is $10. They hear their parents complain and think their parents are just being cheap. To them, coffee is $10 and always has been. But to the parents, maybe it was only $3 when they used to pay for it. Even then, the parents were duped into thinking the price of coffee should be $3 because that's how much it was when they started paying for it. The parents might have called the grandparents cheap for not wanting to pay $3, when the grandparents always used to pay 10 cents for a cup of coffee.

Younger people don't see the trend of inflation because they have only been spending money for a short time. When they see one big inflationary jump, it's easy for them to believe it's the result of greedy corporations. Older people realize inflation is always there, because they have seen prices constantly rise over the course of decades. They know that prices rarely ever come down.

Those in different countries experience things differently. Other countries may have seen sharper or smoother increases in prices. Everything is relative, but perception is everything. You may call something too expensive because you had a price in mind of what it should be, or because you know what else you could get with that same money.

It's hard enough to do this while traveling and using other national currencies. But try doing this with better currencies. How many ounces of silver or gold would you expect to pay for an average lunch? How many Bitcoin or Satoshis (the smallest divisional unit of bitcoin) would you pay?

If you were able to come up with a number, did you do it because you knew exactly what that should cost? Not likely. You probably first considered the prices of these better currencies in dollars or another currency. If the dollar gets inflated into oblivion, that's not going to be a reliable way to understand prices.

People will need to learn to transition. If we throw them into the deep end and expect them to swim, they might just pick it up naturally. But the government will be standing by with a Fed 2.0 life preserver that these people will be ready to grab. Grab it they will, and they make up a majority of the population. These people also have investments tied up in dollars. Whether they have cash hidden under their mattress or in the pages of books around the house, or their retirement fund is invested in government bonds, they will not want to see that value evaporate. All of these people will need to be aware of the transition and how to preserve their wealth.

If you aren't one of these people and don't even know one of these people, they are still an important part of the problem. We need to educate them and help them transition their wealth out of Fed money. Some of these people may already resist the idea because of the political division that's been plaguing this country for decades, but we have to break through that. These are the people who will determine whether the Fed will be replaced with freedom or the Fed 2.0. It is our job to show them the way out.

You don't need to fight with them or alter their beliefs. For many, if you tell them that the dollar is collapsing, they'll think you're crazy. But eventually the government will have to admit that the dollar is failing. If you warn people about this, and tell them what to look for and what to do when they see it, they'll remember it. They may likely joke about it with their friends. This is a good thing, as it burns it into their memory. But when the Fed's collapse becomes too obvious for the government and the media to hide, they will remember. They will suddenly realize that this crazy person who told them to dump their dollars might have been right. They probably won't call you for advice, so make sure you left them with something memorable. When they realize you were right, they should have enough to work with.

Build businesses that help people transition. I know that's easier said than done, especially with the government regulating crypto and gold out of existence. But the more we can do, the better.

During this transition, the dollar won't just disappear. Those notes will be there forever. As people try to get rid of them in exchange for more favorable assets, prices will accelerate further. It's a game of hot potato. If everyone is dumping their dollars, who would sell you their gold or crypto? If they did, they'd be stuck with these notes that are going to be worth even less the next day. The only reason they might take your notes is if they can charge you an outrageous price, then turn around and get rid of them in exchange for another asset, and still expect a profit. The next seller in turn would want to do the same. The movement of dollars will accelerate, and so will the amounts of the transactions. This will follow like a nuclear chain reaction, followed by a complete meltdown.

Think about the systems where investments are stored. If you want to get money out of your retirement account and into crypto or gold, you might have to wait while the dollar is crashing. You'll have to sell some assets and wait for your funds to settle. Then you'll have to wait while it's transferred from one institution to the next. This can all take days, which can be a painfully long time, especially if the dollar is losing more value every hour. Then you have to worry about shortages.

Remember, we're not talking about inflation through printing, we're talking about inflation through disinterest. Trillions in dormant dollars will awaken, ready to be discarded. Valuable assets will skyrocket, even if the printing press is stopped completely. Many people will lose a lot.

The libertarian philosophy is that nobody has an obligation to save another person. While this is technically true, failing to will result in millions of people waking up to absolutely nothing to lose and everything to gain by supporting a new Fed. If you want to change the world, you need to help other people.

Part IV
Starving The Beast

That which is falling should also be pushed.
— Friedrich Nietzsche

Disclaimer

I probably can't reiterate enough that I'm not asking anyone to break the law. I'm simply asking people to use the mechanisms legally available to them. The good news is there are plenty of ways to do this. If you have any concerns, do your own legal research, read through your own contracts, or consult with a lawyer.

Withdrawing Consent

The Federal Reserve looks like a fortress. It has marble columns, armed guards, and the full backing of the U.S. government. It feels untouchable. But here's the secret: its power is not in its walls or weapons. Its power is in *our consent*.

Every time you get paid in dollars, save in dollars, pay taxes in dollars, or deposit them in a bank, you're feeding the machine. Without our participation, the Fed collapses. Withdrawing consent is the first, and most powerful, step toward starving the beast.

Governments always cloak their authority in the illusion of consent. They hold elections, issue notes, pass laws — but at the core, their power comes from people obeying. If enough people stop obeying, the system dies.

Legal tender laws can demand you accept paper dollars, but they can't force you to believe in them. Tax laws can threaten penalties, but they can't extract wealth if everyone finds ways to minimize exposure. They can't even hire enough tax collectors if they don't have anything valuable to pay them with. And their money is only valuable if we accept it. The Fed's system only works as long as we comply.

Every transaction is a vote. When you use Federal Reserve Notes, you are voting for the Fed. When you use alternatives — gold, silver, crypto, barter, even IOUs between neighbors — you are voting against it.

Think of dollars like toxic fuel. Every time you handle them, the machine roars louder. Every time you refuse them, it sputters. If enough of us stop fueling it, the engine stalls.

The federal government is addicted to revenue. Taxes give it the appearance of legitimacy and provide cover for borrowing. But the power of taxation is far more sinister than forcing us to subsidize the government. The total federal tax revenue is $5 trillion per year. The amount of printed notes in circulation is about $2.32 trillion. That means they take almost the entire money supply out of circulation more than twice every year. Think about what that means. Imagine if they stopped spending. They would collect all the nation's money in a year, and we would have no money to spend without somehow earning it back from them.

The government has always been the primary source of money. While the Fed may issue it, the government has to spend it into circulation. When the government taxes it away from us, they have to spend it back into circulation again. This puts the power to direct the money supply in their hands.

Switching to other currencies and eliminating the Fed only addresses one part of the problem. If we allow the government to tax the entire gold, silver and crypto monetary base from us every year, they will still retain the power to direct the entire money supply. All that will have changed is that they can no longer create it at will. But since these currencies are harder for them to control, it becomes a lot more difficult to even do that.

Let's put this in perspective of the left-right paradigm. The left believes that they have little because the wealthy have more. Using this belief, they should understand that the largest collector of the nation's money supply is not the billionaire that's running the big evil tech company. It's the government. The government has direct control over more money than the 100 wealthiest people, all billionaires, combined.

Crash The Fed

First, these can't be compared because most of these billionaires' wealth is fictional, sitting in unrealized gains. Cashing in on any of that would crash markets and reduce their net worth. Second, this is a current valuation of their life's work, where the government taxes, prints, and spends that much every single year. People think milking a few more billionaires will give the government the money it needs to finally give the people something they've been demanding for decades. This is a lie. They have always had the money, but are only interested in helping themselves.

This power of the distribution lies not at the discretion of the people by whom the government purports to serve, but at the discretion of politicians in Washington. If framed properly, the left will understand that we should not be paying taxes. They will support you in ending the Fed using every strategy possible:

- **Use Every Loophole.** The tax code is full of deductions, credits, shelters, and strategies written for the rich. Use them.
- **Structure Your Life.** Form LLCs, trusts, move income into business categories, expense what you legally can.
- **Opt Out.** This is a more controversial method that I have done myself, but it's not for the faint of heart. I have disputed the taxability of all income reported to the IRS and haven't paid a dime in nearly a decade.
- **Push Income Off the Grid.** Side hustles, barter, and informal exchanges are harder to track — and harder to tax. Untraceable transactions like with metals or privacy coins keep the government hands out of your cookie jar.

Every dollar denied to the beast is a dollar it cannot leverage tenfold through the Fed.

The system thrives on guilt. They tell you taxes are "your fair share," that avoiding them is selfish, that accepting benefits is hypocrisy. Don't fall for it, and help your would-be opponents to see the truth.

Remember: this is not a moral government. It is a cartel, using the Fed to enslave you with debt and inflation. Denying it revenue is not cheating your neighbor. It is defending your family, and even your political opponents, from slavery.

Watch How You Spend

Withdrawing consent is not just about saying "no" to the Fed. It's about saying "yes" to alternatives. Every time you trade outside the dollar, you build a parallel economy that competes with the Fed's monopoly.

- **Gold and Silver.** Contracts denominated in metal bypass paper.
- **Crypto.** Bitcoin, Monero, and others create peer-to-peer value flows without central oversight.
- **Local Currencies.** Communities issuing their own credits or notes decentralize control.
- **Barter.** Skills, goods, and services exchanged directly make the Fed irrelevant.

Each transaction outside the dollar is a withdrawal of consent. Each withdrawal weakens the monopoly.

People often say: *"But we have no choice. We're required by law to use dollars and pay taxes."* But law is not the same as compliance. Also, the law is limited, and the government will often tell us we have to do things that we have no legal obligation to. History is full of unjust laws ignored into irrelevance. Prohibition, segregation, apartheid — all ended when people refused to obey.

The Fed is no different. When enough people refuse, enforcement becomes impossible.

Also be aware of who you are giving your money to. Are you giving it to large consolidated corporations? Are these corporations supporting government with funding, information, or power? Think about all the private, for-profit corporations, CEOs, celebrities and others with influence. Think about how they get their money, and how they use their influence to tell people to support government programs. These people often care more about the money than the message, and they learn to stop helping government when they know it will affect their bank accounts.

Withdrawal doesn't require everyone, just enough. Think of it like a boycott. When a critical mass of people divest from the system, the gears grind to a halt. It starts with just a few people. Then it becomes popular and more people join.

- **Individuals** can minimize taxes, hold assets outside the dollar, and transact in alternatives.
- **Businesses** can accept crypto, barter, or local currency.
- **Communities** can organize parallel trade networks.
- **States** can pass laws recognizing gold, silver, or crypto as legal tender, undermining the Fed's monopoly.

Each layer multiplies the effect. Withdrawal scales like a virus — and the Fed has no cure. Support companies that might have a slightly less popular product if they accept alternative currencies. All the little things add up.

Imagine if:
- 10% of Americans shifted savings from banks into gold and crypto.
- 1% of workers, that's over a million, demanded payment in alternatives.
- Communities openly traded in better currencies.

The Fed's illusion of universal consent would shatter. Its monopoly would crack. And the crash would come — not from politicians, but from people quietly refusing to play.

Withdrawing consent takes courage. The system will threaten, guilt, and pressure you to stay in line. But history shows that once enough people say "no," the threats lose power.

We don't need millions storming the Fed's marble halls. We need millions quietly starving it of fuel.

Withdrawing consent is the beginning of liberation. Although it's not often glamorous and rarely makes headlines, it does create business opportunities to profit in helping others. It is also the most powerful weapon we have.

Every time you deny the system your obedience, your money, or your transactions, you weaken it. Every time you trade outside it, you build freedom.

The Fed is not defeated in Washington. It is defeated in kitchens, workshops, farmers' markets, and online trades. It is defeated when enough people refuse to comply.

The crash will not be a law passed. It will be a law ignored. And it begins with you.

Loot the Treasury

Withdrawing consent by paying less in taxes and abstaining from using the Fed's paper or derivatives is only one side of starving the beast. The other side is bleeding it dry.

If you're on the left, you may already support taking money from the government. If you're on the right, you're probably more averse to this, as it causes government debt and taxes to go up. But this is something that benefits both sides equally against the government, when done right.

Consider this. The government's power comes from its ability to direct economic power. Its ability to direct economic power comes from the money it is able to spend from the treasury. That money either comes from printing or taxes. If we stop paying taxes, they will continue to print. They will not give up their power easily.

If the government was designed to serve the people, it is only in the interest of the people to direct that stolen or printed money out of the hands of the politicians and into the hands of the people.

Every check, subsidy, grant, or loan you receive from the government or its banking arms is not "their money" — it is *your stolen labor*, returned in scraps. The question is: what will you do with it?

You can't just take this money and hand it right back to them. If you use it to feed the same consumerist machine, it disappears back into the empire. If you keep it local, redirect it to your family, neighbors, and community, you turn a weapon of enslavement into a tool of liberation.

Give that money back to them only in exchange for things of real value. Leverage it to extract precious metals, crypto and land away from government possession. In the end, when we hold all the real assets and the government and Fed hold only their own useless notes, we will have returned sovereign power to the people.

This strategy often comes as a shock to libertarians, conservatives, anti-Fed-eralists, and right-wingers, but bear with me.

You should never feel guilty about taking government money. You shouldn't be mad at people who take money from the government. They aren't your enemy. Handouts do not increase taxes. Increased taxes produce handouts. Remember, whatever the government takes from us, they must spend back into the economy, or we will be left with nothing.

The tragedy is not that people collect benefits. The tragedy is that most waste them on cheap imports, debt payments, taxes, or luxuries that leave the community. That's why Washington doesn't mind handing out checks — most of it cycles back into the same corporate cartels, and the Fed.

But when you deliberately capture that flow and *keep it in your economy*, you deny the system its recycling loop. You slow the Fed's machine and strengthen your community at the same time. In fact, we need to increase the amount of money that's paid into communities from the government. This doesn't increase taxes, this decreases the money available for other projects that are used to launder money back into powerful pockets.

I am not advocating socialism, though there are similarities. Socialism would be the planned redistribution of wealth from one group of people to another. I am not advocating for more taxes, just to release what has already been stolen. The intent of socialism is to be permanent, centrally planned, and force everyone to become dependent on the government.

Some will say that if you give the government the power to feed you, you give it the power to starve you. I disagree. I say that only if you *depend* on the government to feed you, do you give it the power to starve you. The government has created many of their welfare programs in such a way that it traps people in, forcing them to become dependent, preventing them from leaving. To break this system does not take reform, because remember, we can't trust legislators to fix this problem for us.

Instead, we need to guide people who are receiving those benefits to join us in ending the Fed.

Don't Call Them Leeches – Teach Them

It's easy to look at neighbors cashing benefits and sneer: "leeches." That's what the system wants us to think. Division keeps us weak.

Instead, we need to reframe: "That's our money coming back. Now let's use it wisely."

The better path is education. Show others how to:
- Spend benefits locally instead of on corporate chains.
- Use subsidies to build assets instead of funding waste.
- Invest in tools, skills, and community trade.

The difference between a parasite and a patriot is intent. If you're using those resources to prepare for collapse and strengthen your neighbors, you are draining the empire and investing in freedom.

These people are in the position to qualify for the legal extraction of money from the government. Don't fight them. Let them have it. Encourage it. Ask that in exchange they support you paying fewer taxes.

But don't stop there. Give them more. Teach them how to invest. Encourage them to start side hustles. Teach them that serving the community is the best way to build wealth. Show them the right way to build wealth while keeping it far enough away to not take away their benefits. The same methods that people use for sheltering their money from taxes could be used to shelter people from having their benefits taken away.

Support debt forgiveness for college loans. If someone owes money to the government and overnight that debt disappears, that's just like a subsidy. Let them have it. This will not increase your taxes. Instead, it will increase government debt. But that is not your debt. You don't have to repay that. Stop thinking about your taxes as somehow matching government expenses. They haven't been able to balance their books in decades, and when they have it's been for a very short time. If you free up money from one place, they'll just spend it somewhere else. They will spend whatever they want on top of that, regardless of revenue. They can do that because they can print. The more they print, the sooner we get rid of the Fed.

There is no reason for there to be a war between the haves and the have-nots. At the end of the day, we are all victims of the oppression of the Fed. Instead of fighting over the scraps, we need to work together. If you have more than others, help them up to your level.

If you want to do this because your faith agrees with it, that's great. If you want to do this because you understand they are suffering more than you, that's also great. But don't think that this is a socialist obligation. Under socialism, the threat is that if you don't help them you'll go to prison. The threat here is that if you don't help them, the Fed will continue to reign over you with immense power.

If you can't convince yourself to do it for others, do it for yourself.

Milk Big Corporations

Health insurance is another racket that, just like the Fed, is run by a powerful group of people with a great amount of power leveraged over the government. They use congress to pass laws that serve to boost their profits, transferring a great amount of wealth from the hard-working public to the elite.

In 2010, The Affordable Care Act, also known as ObamaCare or RomneyCare, became law. This bill promised to solve everyone's medical problems, with cheaper insurance and less money out of pocket. Americans quickly learned that they had been duped when their cost of healthcare exploded nearly overnight.

One of the problems in the bill was that it included a profit cap on insurance companies. While this sounded like a great way to force premiums down, it did the opposite.

It's a simple math problem. If you are making $1 billion on a business with a 50% profit margin, how do you make the same $1 billion on a business with only a 10% profit margin. The answer is simple – increase your expenses and increase your revenue.

The insurance companies were happy to do this, knowing that their customers couldn't just drop their policies. When the law was first passed, it included an individual mandate, which required every single American to have health insurance or face hefty fines. (It turned out to be a false threat, but I'll save that explanation for another book.) Since people were afraid to cancel their health insurance, they would just pay the higher rates. Businesses who offered health insurance to their employees would take on most of the cost.

Now that their premiums were much higher, the insurance companies would have to spend a lot more. Since they couldn't make more people sign up or tell them to get more procedures, they told providers to charge them a lot more. Yes, insurance companies told the people who were billing them to charge them a lot more. They needed to spend the money to keep their profits up.

This sounds counterintuitive, but let's do some basic math with an imaginary insurance company. Before the ACA, they were making $1 billion in profit by charging $2 billion in premiums and spending $1 billion in benefits. After the ACA, they wanted to keep their same profits, so they increased their premiums five-fold to $10 billion. Now they have to spend $9 billion on the same number of policyholders. But do they need nine times as many procedures done? Not likely. Instead, they tell the providers to bill nine times more and they'll happily pay it. The insurance company is still making their $1 billion profit.

What happens if the providers don't charge more? Imagine they are only able to get their payouts up to $5 billion. Now they have a $5 billion profit, which is 50%. But they can only have 10%. The profit cap says that if their profits exceed the cap, they have to return that money to their customers, reducing their profit to 10%. That means that on $5 billion in payouts, they can only keep about $5.5 billion of their premiums. They have to return $4.5 billion to their customers, and they only have about $500 million in profit – half of what they could have had if they had just paid out more to the providers.

Why don't they just help more people instead of denying claims? I can't answer this for sure, but I can speculate. There are only so many providers, and most of them are backlogged. Patients trying to book appointments with doctors are left waiting for months. If everything was approved, those lines would likely get longer. The longer it takes to serve a patient, the longer it takes to bill them. If they don't get billed until the next year, the insurance company can't take the profit until the next year. That also means they are going to be returning more money to their policyholders.

Interestingly, most providers are willing to work with people who don't have insurance. They know that their rates are inflated beyond what most people can or will pay. Most providers will offer a cash price that is one tenth of what they charge the insurance company. But they can't just give two different prices. Two prices would expose the entire fraud that they are price gouging the insurance companies. Instead, they have to first bill you the same amount, and sometimes only when you ask, give you special discounts. But there's another gotcha – the insurance companies have contractual gag orders that forbid providers from telling you their cash price or negotiating with you, once they know that you have insurance.

So how do we use all this to our advantage? Consider this – you go to a doctor or a pharmacy, and you tell them you are paying cash. You get the cash price, and you pay with your credit card. You take the bill, send it to your insurance company, and have them reimburse you for the cost of the services you received. You just saved the insurance company a lot of money. At first glance this sounds like a silly idea. If you were price gouged on premiums, why not just make them pay? Because if enough people do this, they will be forced to pay a portion of the premiums to all their policyholders.

Different policies have different rules, so check with your policy before acting on this information. But doing this is a great way to reduce the cost of healthcare, and keep money in your community instead of sending it off to the wealthy elites.

Forcing Out The Gold

There is a popular conspiracy theory that recently had 15 minutes of fame in the mainstream. That is that there is no gold in Fort Knox. The vault is supposed to hold about 4.5 tons of gold, but there has not been a full audit since the 1950s. A few times since, congress was allowed to see the gold, or other inspections were made, but there was never a full audit. Conspiracy theorists claim that during some of these audits, it was noted that seals were broken on certain containers, but that their contents were not counted.

Crash The Fed

In February 2025, just after Trump took office for his second term, he was working closely with Elon Musk on a project called D.O.G.E. – the Department of Government Efficiency. The purpose of this program was to sniff out government waste and cut it out. While promoting this, Musk mentioned that it was probably a good idea to audit Fort Knox. To this date, nothing has come of that.

Before Nixon "closed the gold window" in 1971, that gold would have been used to buy back dollars from foreign countries that received them in exchange for exports. This would prevent those countries from dumping dollars on the open exchange and crashing their value – to their own detriment.

What caused this? If other countries would have just held onto their money, there would be no need to stop sending them gold. Nixon accused "international money speculators" of trying to undermine the dollar by taking all the U.S.' gold. But there was no speculation, it was only holders of promises trying to redeem them.

Imagine if someone pleaded with you to accept an IOU in exchange for your hard work. When you tell them you're ready to accept payment, they accuse you of being a speculator and refuse to pay. This is exactly what the government did.

Why? What did they have to gain? Were they trying to hoard the gold for other reasons? Or had they made more promises than they could deliver?

Because the government was printing money in excess of the amount of gold in their vaults, it's very possible that they foresaw a bank run on Fort Knox. If the countries holding FRNs wanted their gold, the government would not have had enough. It's just like a busted Ponzi scheme. Remember, the notes are backed by bonds, and the bonds are backed by notes. But most other countries were expecting the notes to be backed by gold, as they ultimately don't want either form of paper.

The U.S. can get away with printing an unlimited supply of money, as long as the notes are circulating within their own country. At home, people treat it like money. But once that money leaves the country into economies that have their own currencies, it's only valuable if they can exchange it or redeem it. It's estimated that between 50% and 65% of all FRNs are outside the U.S.

The U.S. claims to have about 4.5 tons of gold in Fort Knox, and about 9 tons of gold total. The Fed claims they are holding about 6.5 tons of gold, although they claim they are just holding it for governments around the world.

So what happens if these governments come asking for their gold again? It's possible that the Fed, with the U.S. government's protection, refuses to release the gold. But how long can they stand on this gold and claim to be the most powerful bank and government in the world? Only as long as we keep giving value to their fake promises.

Imagine what happens when the dollar fails. We're talking complete failure, well beyond hyperinflation. When they can't print enough money to pay their bills because people just don't want it, the government will have no choice but to start spending its gold.

Use Every Opportunity You Can

The state hands out endless programs — not out of generosity, but as bait to secure compliance. Take the bait, but don't swallow the hook.

If you are already in the category of receiving welfare benefits or government money, that's great! Keep it going and step up your game!

- **FHA Loans.** Use subsidized mortgages not for speculation, but to acquire property that can serve your community. Remember, if the dollar crashes, these loans may just disappear.
- **Student Grants.** Take them, but use them to build marketable skills and networks that endure beyond the collapse. Don't waste them on useless courses. Stay away from loans that have unrealistic terms. Start new schools that accept government grants and loans.
- **Business Loans and Credits.** Funnel them into real, tangible goods — tools, equipment, and workshops, all with the purpose of helping the effort to draw money away from the government and the Fed, and into communities, alternative monetary systems, and other forms of independence.

Every time you intercept one of these cash streams and lock it into real value, you weaken the system, crush dependence, and help to liberate the public.

A New Model for Real Estate

One of the most powerful strategies is to flip real estate from a profit-driven model into a community-driven one.

Most investors see property as passive income, a way to squeeze tenants and extract rent. That mindset mirrors the Fed itself — parasitic, focused on long-term dependency.

Instead, imagine this:
- You use FHA or other low-interest loans to acquire houses or apartments.
- You offer them back to neighbors through *rent-to-own* arrangements.
- Families who could never qualify for bank loans now have a path to ownership.
- You earn modestly, but more importantly, you've anchored wealth in your community.
- Use the opportunity to teach your tenants about being responsible with money and building wealth for their family.

This is not charity. It is strategic. Every strong household you help create becomes a partner in the parallel economy. Every family that owns their home is harder for the Fed to crush - not to mention a thorn in the side of private equity firms like BlackRock that are trying to consolidate single family homes and turn the country into a nation of renters.

Their wealth is your wealth. You gain something even more valuable than passive income: you gain resilient customers, allies, and future educators who will spread financial literacy. And this isn't charity. You aren't losing money on this. You might even be able to reduce your taxes on this. You might even be able to arrange it to operate as a non-profit organization.

Economic activity always requires customers. If your neighbors are broke, your business fails. If they're strong, your ventures thrive. Strengthening them strengthens you.

By acting as a bridge — a "straw man" against predatory banks — you can give others the opportunity to buy homes, build businesses, and prepare for collapse. While Wall Street siphons wealth upward, you reverse the flow downward into real communities.

And as soon as you have those dollars, get rid of them as fast as you can. Use them to import real wealth into your community – metals, crypto, or other more valuable assets. Use it to localize production of anything from food to water to energy. Don't just put that money in the bank to rot.

It's not just about real estate. The same principles apply everywhere:
- **Food.** Subsidies or benefits spent at farmers' markets keep farms alive.
- **Energy.** Grants or credits used for solar panels strengthen grid independence.
- **Education.** Loans or stipends used to train in trades or survival skills create long-term resilience.

The key is intent. Whatever stream comes your way, grab it, and lock it into something real, local, and enduring.

Breaking the Shame Cycle

The system thrives on two lies:
1. That you should feel guilty for "taking" money back.
2. That others who do so are parasites.

Both are designed to keep us divided and compliant. The truth is simple: *every benefit, every loan, every subsidy is already yours*. Taking it back and using it strategically is not theft. It is reclamation.

Starving the beast is not just about withholding consent. It is also about reclaiming stolen wealth and turning it into strength.

Don't feel guilty for intercepting government money. Feel guilt only if you waste it or send it back to the government. Every check you capture and reinvest locally is a victory. Every loan turned into assets for your neighbors is a strike against the empire.

This is the mindset shift: stop thinking like a subject, start thinking like a strategist. The Fed will fall. The question is whether we'll be ready with strong communities, or whether we'll let the state rebuild Fed 2.0 in the ruins.

The time to take back what's yours is now.

Trading Paper for Value

Dollars feel like wealth because it's what we've always known. You work, you're paid in dollars, you save them, you spend them. But at its core, a Federal Reserve Note is not wealth — it is a claim against the future, backed by debt and fraud.

Every day you hold one, it loses value. Inflation is not an accident — it is the design. The dollar was never meant to preserve your labor. It was meant to siphon it away.

That's why dollars must be treated like a *hot potato*. They have some short-term utility, but the longer you hold them, the more you lose. The goal is simple: **get as much as you can, and get rid of it as quickly as you can — but trade it for something real.**

The Fed trains you to think "savings" means dollars in a bank account. They even try to bribe you with pathetic interest rates. But a dollar saved is a dollar devalued.

- In 1970, $100 could buy a full cart of groceries. Today, it barely covers a handful of items.
- In 1913, $100 had the purchasing power of over $2,700 today.

If you had saved those dollars, you lost. If you had traded them for gold, silver, land, or even stock, you won.

Savings in dollars is not security — it is slow-motion theft.

In the past, people have worried about the solvency of banks. They'll say "take your money out of the bank," as if that's the place you're going to lose it. But when you take your money out, you're just getting FRNs. These are just banknotes. That means that your money is still in the bank!

They control the value, which means they control your wealth and your economic power, which means they control you. You can't take your money out of the bank at the ATM. You have to get rid of your banknotes too!

The Hot Potato Rule

Here's the rule: **treat dollars like a hot potato.**
- Get as many as you can.
- Hold only what you need for immediate survival.
- Convert the rest into real assets before it burns your hand.

This doesn't mean reckless spending. It means strategic conversion: turning toxic paper into things the Fed cannot print. There are unlimited options.

1. **Gold and Silver**

   Timeless stores of value. They preserve wealth through every collapse. Unlike fiat, they cannot be devalued by decree. If you really believe government issued money has some sort of higher status, buy U.S. minted gold and silver coins.

2. **Bitcoin and Crypto**

   Decentralized, censorship-resistant, borderless. Not all coins matter — Bitcoin and privacy coins like Monero are strongest for survival and trade.

3. **Land and Real Estate**

   Dirt doesn't disappear. Soil grows food, property shelters families, and ownership outlasts fiat.

4. **Tools and Equipment**

   Machinery, workshops, hardware. A lathe, a generator, or a truck can produce real value when dollars collapse. Don't cheap out, some tools are built to last or be repairable and may cost a little bit more.

5. **Food and Energy**

   Rice, beans, canned goods, solar panels, wood stoves. What you can eat or burn has real value. Don't stockpile things that will expire.

6. **Community Investments**

Loan your neighbor cash for equipment, buy into local ventures, or start barter networks. When the dollar dies, the relationships survive.

7. **Stocks in Productive Businesses**
All stocks carry risk, but some stocks can withstand an economic crash. A company that makes food, energy, or tools will always have value. Businesses that make luxuries may fail.

Invest in assets, not IOUs. Treasury bonds are the worst place you can be. They are nothing but paper promises to repay in more paper. Holding Treasuries, whether directly or in your 401(k), is literally betting on the Fed. When the Fed collapses, those "safe assets" will be worthless.

Take Custody

I mentioned before that holding assets in a centralized system makes them an easy target by the government. There are many options for metals and crypto that allow you to buy and sell online. The trouble is that you'll never hold onto these for yourself. While they do belong to you, it's just like holding money in a bank account. The government has easy access. A third party is your only line of defense, and they are not likely to stand up to the government on your behalf.

This is called custodial holding or a custodial account. Someone else is in physical possession of your investment. Noncustodial holding would mean that you are the person in direct possession.

With custodial holdings, assets are sometimes leveraged. If a company isn't careful, it can find themselves in an insolvent position. When this happens, the company goes out of business and account holders can lose their assets.

Hedge your risks. Vaulted gold is often stored in a safe place that makes it difficult for common criminals to break in. It's more secure against this type of theft than keeping it around the house. But keeping it at home in a safe place can protect you against other kinds of theft, like government confiscation. Safety deposit boxes where the bank doesn't inventory your assets is another option with pros and cons.

Keep in mind, the government doesn't have to be after your money for you to lose it from a custodian. Sometimes the government targets a financial institution for some arbitrary accusation of money laundering or simple noncompliance. The institutions often follow every law as best as they can, but the government often takes down innocent targets. Even if the end result is that everyone is acquitted of all crimes, institutions' reputations can be damaged and lose stability by paying massive legal fees. You aren't the target, but your vault becomes the target, and you end up with the loss.

Taking custody on your own creates other problems that you should be aware of. If you're going to be trading for metals, learn how to tell real coins apart from fake ones. Watch out for scams such as scammers selling counterfeits online. Either buy from a reputable dealer online or buy in person where you can test the coins yourself.

When it comes to crypto, noncustodial holding is far better than leaving it in an exchange. But there are safe ways to do this. Wallets can be hot or cold. Hot wallets are kept in your cell phone or laptop and have direct access to your private keys. Unfortunately this makes them more vulnerable to attacks by hackers. Cold wallets are stored in USB sticks or Bluetooth devices that keep your keys out of your other devices. When you're ready to send crypto, you'll initiate a transaction in your phone and use the device to confirm it.

There are still many precautions to take into consideration. Lose your seed keys and you won't have access to any of your crypto. If someone steals your seed phrase, they'll be able to take everything. This means security becomes your own responsibility, but it makes it far more difficult for anyone, including the government, to get their hands on your money.

It's important to educate yourself on the pros and cons of the various types of accounts and understand which is best for your personal situation.

Markets Will Skyrocket

As you get rid of your FRNs, they make their way into markets, forcing prices up quickly. This is a basic law of economics. What markets? When you save your wealth by buying gold, silver, and crypto, you're putting more money into those markets.

Some people falsely believe that when markets go up that money is gained, and when they go down, money is lost. They are looking at the market cap, or market capitalization – the total value of the asset at the price the market currently shows. But this is a misdirection.

Recall when we talked about markets. There isn't really a market price. There is only a last price. The price which the last transaction was made, does not mean that any of the future transactions will be above or below that price.

Money is not created or destroyed in these markets. I have seen too many people make this claim. When markets are up they say that wealth is being created. When markets plummet, they say wealth is being wiped out or eliminated. But that's not the case. It is simply exchanged. One person trades fiat for another person's gold or crypto. The more people who want to sell, the easier it will be for buyers to come in with lower offers. If one person makes a $1 billion gain, someone else loses $1 billion – at least on paper.

Imagine if the gold market were locked off today to where no new gold or dollars could enter or leave the exchange. Those holding either gold or dollars would continue to speculate and trade. Prices would go up and down depending on who wants to buy or sell. But at the end of the day, there would still be the exact same amount of gold and fiat in the market.

When we see markets rise, many will say that it's a bubble ready to crash. This will happen from time to time as people overinvest. Eventually, someone will want to take their profit by selling the asset. This causes a small price dip followed by panic selling by everyone else. Eventually the bubble pops. But this isn't always the case. Think about how that starts – by someone wanting to sell a lot of their stock to cash out. That means that someone wants a lot of fiat. If the dollar is crashing, this will not likely be the case. If someone does want to cash out, they will likely not settle for lower prices. The price will also recover quickly, as more new money continues to flood the market.

When it comes to stocks, metals, or crypto, we should not look at their value in terms of dollars. Doing so means that when the dollar becomes worthless, we will be looking at charts that don't make any sense. An ounce of gold on a gold vs dollar chart will look like it's worth trillions, or some insanely large number. It will look as though anyone who holds an ounce today has an insane amount of wealth. But that gold won't really be worth much more than it is now. These numbers will be meaningless.

Investing in these assets isn't about making free money by holding onto something valuable, it's about holding onto something whose value won't deteriorate. When you buy assets like gold and crypto, you are tipping the scales to the side of buys. You are competing with other buyers and forcing the prices up. But you are also getting rid of dollars, and forcing their value down.

Those who are foolishly getting out of those markets will be left with the dying currency.

Holding FRNs Increases Their Value

Think about the opposite. If everyone is chasing FRNs, there are more people buying them than selling them. You can buy FRNs with just about anything – gold, silver, crypto, food, or even your labor. The more people chasing after these FRNs, the more value they have. If you really wanted those FRNs badly, you might be willing to accept fewer of them for the things you have to trade. That means the FRNs are more valuable.

The more you collect and store FRNs, the more you help the Fed kick the can down the road and keep its scam going. Get rid of those FRNs, and even bypass them altogether by accepting alternate currencies if you can.

Every dollar you hold validates their monopoly. It gives them time to keep the scam running.

A great analogy is a real world event that happened with GameStop stock. In early 2021, a group of retail investors called WallStreetBets began buying heavily shorted GME stock, driving its price up more than 1,000%. Institutional investors were counting on the struggling business to fail and the stock prices to plummet.

Their shorts meant that they would sell stock they didn't have at a prearranged price, lower than the current trading price. It's a gamble. Their expectation was that the stock would fall even lower than the price they sold it at, and when it was time to deliver the stock, they would buy it cheap and make a profit. But since all the retail traders were buying up all the stock and refusing to sell, the institutional investors had no choice but to buy the stocks at sky-high prices, losing billions. This made the stock of the struggling company worth far more than the company was actually worth. Although the bubble eventually popped, this went on for quite some time.

GameStop teaches us that if enough of the little guys work together, they can transfer a large amount of wealth away from powerful institutions. The value of assets is determined by the desire of people to buy or sell them. Massively hoarding an asset will inflate its price.

Consider how many of us are hoarding assets that push the value of the dollar up. Every dollar in your savings account, and every treasury bond in your safe or in your retirement fund, is a small pillar supporting the inflated value of the dollar. Hundreds of millions of people wanting to get as many as they can will artificially inflate the value of the dollar. It doesn't matter if they are actual notes in paper, bonds, or fractional reserve derivatives.

The dollar, like GameStop, is already struggling to survive. The only reason it's perceived to be valuable is because so many of us treat it like it's valuable. This artificially inflates its value. But as soon as we decide to stop holding, the bubble will pop, just like it did with GameStop.

Why Speed Matters

The Fed's theft is exponential. A dollar held too long doesn't just dissolve slowly — it can vanish overnight in crisis. Ask Argentines in 2001, or Zimbabweans in 2008. One week their money bought groceries. The next, it bought nothing.

Don't assume you'll have time to "cash out" later. The collapse will not be gradual and polite. It will be sudden and brutal. The time to convert is before panic hits.

This isn't just about you. Communities can adopt the hot potato mindset too. When benefits checks arrive, keep them circulating locally instead of at corporate chains. When subsidies flow, use them to build assets — gardens, workshops, solar. When loans come, flip them into durable goods or housing that strengthens your neighbors.

The Fed wants those dollars to circle back into its system. Instead, we must intercept them, strip them of value, and turn them into resilience.

Withdrawing consent requires discipline. It's tempting to sit on a pile of cash "just in case." It feels safer. It feels empowering. But in reality, it is the riskiest thing you can do.

Set a rule:
- Keep only what you need for 1–2 months of emergencies.
- Convert the rest into assets as soon as possible.
- Review regularly — if you're sitting on excess cash, move it.

This discipline keeps you ahead of collapse, not crushed by it.

When the Fed finally falls, paper dollars will die with it. Government debts, pensions, and promises will vanish too. But gold, land, food, skills, and community will remain.

Those who practiced the hot potato rule will wake up holding real value. Those who clutched paper will wake up empty-handed.

The dollar is not wealth. It is a liability dressed up as money. It's an IOU from a private bank and the government – both of who will blame the other when you come looking for fulfillment. Neither will ever pay what they owe. The longer you hold it, the easier it is for them to say "that was a long time ago".

The path to survival is simple: **get as much as you can, and get rid of it as quickly as you can — by trading it for real value.** Every day you delay, the hot potato burns a little more of your future away.

Don't be the last one holding the bag. Be the one who flipped it into freedom.

Most of the glamorous luxuries that we are conditioned to waste our money on for community approval are ultimately supporting the Fed. There are many great companies out there that are worthy of our support, but they are hard to tell apart. Some started off great, but got so big that they were purchased by private equity firms that consolidate wealth and provide only to the same wealthy elites that run the Fed.

Part V
Packing The Parachute

You never change things
by fighting the existing reality.
To change something, build a new model
that makes the old one obsolete.
— Buckminster Fuller

Building Parallel Systems

Starving the beast weakens the Fed, but survival requires more than tearing down. It requires building up. If all we do is crash the dollar, we'll create chaos. If we build parallel systems now, collapse becomes a transition — from fraud to freedom.

Parallel systems are not theoretical. They already exist. Farmers' markets, barter circles, crypto exchanges, community currencies, co-ops — these are seeds of independence. The task is to water them, expand them, and connect them into a functioning economy that outlasts the Fed.

Nature survives by redundancy. You have two lungs, two kidneys, and a backup system for almost every critical function. Our economy should be the same.

Right now, we have only one system: the dollar. Most of us have one company that gives us electricity, and one grocery store that feeds us. If any of these collapse, everything tied to them collapses too. Parallel systems give us redundancy. They ensure that when the Fed's monopoly fails, life goes on.

Food is the most obvious starting point. Supermarkets depend on long supply chains vulnerable to currency shocks. Local production breaks that dependency.

- **Farmers' Markets.** Direct trade between growers and buyers cuts out dollar-denominated middlemen.
- **Community Supported Agriculture (CSA).** Prepaid memberships provide farmers stable revenue and families reliable food.

- **Backyard and Urban Gardens.** Even small-scale growing reduces reliance on fragile chains.
- **Food Co-ops.** Community-owned grocery stores keep profits local and decisions democratic.

These larger, centralized systems depend on a stable currency. Supermarkets generally have a low profit margin. Their high volume is the only reason they thrive. Low profit margin means that they can't gamble with price fluctuations. If they buy a thing for 90 cents and sell it for a dollar, they need to know that they can buy it again from their supplier for 90 cents. Yes, they can increase the prices on their shelves, but the next restock comes *after* the sale. The more uncertainty in pricing, the higher they have to increase their prices.

The supermarkets aren't the only ones dealing with this issue. Every step along the supply chain has to deal with it. This means that they are virtually forced to use FRNs because their entire chain uses them. Nobody in that chain can gamble with alternative currencies.

Local farmers, on the other hand, can. They might still need to purchase from suppliers, but less of their operation is dependent on that. There are fewer hands that have to change money to get that food from the local farm to your table. That means that these transactions will be easier to switch to alternative currencies. Every tomato grown in a backyard or bought from a neighbor is a blow to the Fed's centralized supply system.

Not only that, but as the dollar becomes increasingly unstable, markets with long supply chains will start to see the effects of using unstable currencies. Now that they have forced themselves to stick with a single currency for predictability, the loss of that predictability could be disastrous.

Energy is the lifeblood of an economy. When dollars collapse, so will large-scale fuel imports. Parallel systems mean local power.
- **Solar Panels.** Even small-scale rooftop systems provide independence.
- **Microgrids.** Communities can pool solar, wind, or hydro for shared resilience.
- **Wood, Biofuel, and Generators.** Old-school backups remain valuable.

Crash The Fed

The point is not 100% independence for everyone — it's layers of redundancy. The more nodes of local power, the less fragile the system.

The Fed's greatest weapon is its monopoly on money. Breaking it requires parallel currencies.
- **Gold and Silver.** Always accepted, always valuable.
- **Crypto.** Bitcoin for global trade, privacy coins for local resilience.
- **Local Currencies.** Localized organizations can issue and oversee local currencies or credit systems to keep trade flowing when dollars fail.
- **Barter Networks.** Direct exchange of goods and services bypasses fiat entirely.

Parallel money systems don't have to replace the dollar overnight. They just need to exist so that when the dollar falters, trade continues.

One of the biggest drains on communities is rent and mortgages flowing to distant banks. Parallel systems keep property control local.
- **Community Land Trusts.** Land held in trusts for local use, not speculation.
- **Rent-to-Own Models.** Neighbors helping neighbors into ownership instead of enriching banks.
- **Local Financing Pools.** Communities lending to each other instead of begging Wall Street, paying them outrageous interest rates, and risking losing everything in default.

The house you live in should enrich your community, not the Federal Reserve or some giant corporate bank.

Universities are bloated, debt-fueled institutions. Real education thrives in parallel.
- **Trade Schools and Workshops.** Skills training outside the debt trap.
- **Homeschooling and Co-ops.** Families pooling resources for education.
- **Skill-Sharing Networks.** Local classes on gardening, repair, finance, medicine.

Knowledge is wealth. Sharing it freely builds resilience faster than any subsidy.

When the dollar collapses, insurance-based healthcare will collapse too. Communities can prepare now.
- **Direct Primary Care.** Membership-based doctor-patient models.
- **Local Clinics.** Funded by communities, not insurers.
- **Alternative Medicine.** Herbal, naturopathic, and holistic practices.
- **Mutual Aid Health Funds.** Neighbors pooling resources for emergencies.

Medicine should be about healing, not billing codes. Parallel health systems reclaim that truth.

Scaling Parallel Systems

Some think parallel systems are fringe. But look closer: they already sustain millions.
- Credit unions vs. big banks.
- Farmers' markets vs. Walmart.
- Bitcoin vs. PayPal.
- Homeschooling vs. state schools.

The question is not whether they exist, but whether we will expand them fast enough.

Parallel systems are not just technical — they are cultural. People need to see them as normal, not weird. That requires:
- **Language.** Stop calling it "alternative" — call it "better."
- **Celebration.** Farmers' markets as festivals. Local currencies as badges of pride.
- **Education.** Teaching kids barter, saving in gold, coding crypto wallets.

Culture sustains economies. Build culture around independence.

Parallel systems also act as a shield against Fed 2.0. If the state rolls out a CBDC, the only real defense is already-functioning alternatives. If people have no choice but to comply, they will. If they already have a network of barter, gold, and crypto, they can refuse.

Crash The Fed

Parallel systems are not optional. They are necessary for survival.

The Fed will collapse. The only question is whether we collapse with it, or whether we land on the safety net we've built.

Parallel systems are that net. They are the new economy, built in the shadow of the old. Every dollar you convert, every tomato you grow, every trade you make outside fiat — these are stitches in the fabric of freedom.

We don't need to wait for permission. We don't need to wait for the current system to collapse. We can build now. And when the paper empire falls, we'll be ready.

Local Currencies

Many books about money push the idea that money was created as a means for exchange to replace barter. There is some truth to this, but it misses a step. The first money was a promise to deliver something that was not available yet. If I wanted to barter with you, but I hadn't yet harvested the crop with which I would buy your livestock, I could write you a note. This note would be an IOU for my crops when they became available. If you changed your mind, you could take that IOU and trade it with someone else. That other person could always come to me when my crops were ready, and buy them with that IOU. When the IOU is redeemed, the IOU is destroyed.

This is an important illustration that money is a promise, and not always created from nothing. Its value is in the fact that there is a direct underlying substance for which it can be traded.

Local currencies can work in the same way. A small group of people can get together and create a new currency. When people say they would like to use this currency to ditch the dollar, they can pledge some of their future goods or services as backing for the currency. In giving this IOU to the issuing group, they would receive some local currency. They could then take this currency to others in the community and buy what the other has already pledged. The vendor who receives the money could either keep this money to buy more from someone else, or they could take it back to the managers of the currency to buy back and destroy their IOU, eliminating their debt.

This and similar models of local currencies have been tested in small communities and colleges with great results. Not every community has the same values or level of trust, so every local currency may be different – but that's what makes them great. They can best serve the needs of each community because they are created by the communities with their exact needs in mind.

Alternative Financial Networks

Food, energy, and housing are critical — but without a way to exchange value, economies freeze. That's why the Fed's most dangerous weapon is its monopoly on money and payment systems. It doesn't just control the dollar; it controls the pipes through which dollars flow.

Breaking free requires building *parallel financial networks* that allow people to trade, save, and invest outside the Fed's reach.

- **Banks.** Fragile, debt-driven, and loyal to regulators and tax collectors. Bail-ins and freezes are inevitable.
- **Payment Processors.** Visa, Mastercard, PayPal, ACH, SWIFT, FedWire — all choke points, quick to freeze accounts when politics demand it.
- **Wall Street.** The casino that siphons Main Street's savings into elite hands.

Depending on these systems in collapse is suicide. We need alternatives now.

- **Gold and Silver.** The oldest financial network. Coins and bullion circulate as trust-based assets beyond inflation. Goldbacks are privately issued, thin sheets of real gold with a protective coating meant to replace notes.
- **Crypto.** Bitcoin for global settlement, privacy coins like Monero for local resilience. Decentralized exchanges (DEXs) bypass banking choke points. Decentralized Finance (DeFi) for lending and borrowing.
- **Local Currencies.** Ithaca HOURS, BerkShares, or digital community credits. Keep trade flowing even if national money collapses.

- **Time Banks.** Hours of labor exchanged directly, bypassing fiat entirely.
- **Peer-to-Peer Crypto Payments.** Wallet-to-wallet, no bank approval.
- **Mesh Networks.** Digital infrastructure that routes payments without centralized servers.
- **Paper Vouchers.** Old-fashioned but effective — print redeemable community notes.

The point isn't technology for its own sake. The point is redundancy: multiple ways to pay when the Fed's rails fail.

Alternative Savings and Credit

Credit unions. Member-owned and locally focused, credit unions are often less captured by big-bank interests because they're governed by members, not distant shareholders. They tend to be smaller, less profit-driven, and more willing to make relationship-based loans; some even use private deposit insurance instead of the FDIC, giving them operational flexibility. That local governance makes them natural partners for community finance experiments — but most remain fiat-based institutions. To become true building blocks of a Fed-bypassing system, credit unions need to open their operations to new ideas. They can start by holding hard assets or crypto as collateral, create gold-backed savings accounts, and offer loan products explicitly denominated or partially collateralized in non-fiat stores of value.

Mutual aid funds. These are horizontal, community-run pools where people contribute small amounts to provide emergency grants or interest-free loans when members face hardships. They require simple governance rules, transparency, and trust mechanisms (rotating administrators, public ledgers, or multisig wallets) to scale without bureaucracy. As an alternative finance tool they keep capital circulating inside communities, reduce dependence on external credit, and build social resilience — especially if mutual aid pools coordinate with local lenders or credit unions for larger needs, or if they diversify holdings into durable goods or precious metals to protect against fiat erosion.

Hard-asset savings. Storing wealth in metals, durable tools, long-shelf food, or land is the classic anti-inflation strategy: these assets don't evaporate when central banks expand base money. Practical steps include stacking small, auditable amounts of physical gold/silver, creating community-accessible tool libraries, pre-purchasing bulk food supplies, and buying fractional shares of local productive land. Hard assets anchor value locally and reduce the need to convert labor into fiat holdings that can be diluted by monetary policy — and if community institutions (credit unions, mutual funds, co-ops) hold and insure these assets, they can use them as real collateral for loans rather than just paper promises.

Local lending circles. Small groups agree to rotate pooled payments so members get lump sums when needed — a time-tested, zero-interest credit mechanism used worldwide. They require minimal overhead, rely on social enforcement, and can be adapted to use non-fiat denominators like gold grams, stablecoin units, or tokenized shares of community assets. Lending circles bypass Wall Street's intermediaries by creating direct credit paths among neighbors. When linked to local institutions that accept alternative collateral, they become a bridge between grassroots savings and larger, regulated lending capacity.

Each of these pieces solves a different failure of fiat banking: credit unions provide a regulated, member-centric system; mutual aid funds give emergency liquidity without debt; hard assets preserve purchasing power across crises; and lending circles supply short-term credit without predatory fees. Combined, they keep capital circulating locally rather than leaking to Wall Street, build real resilience to monetary inflation, and give communities the infrastructure to transact, borrow, and save on their own terms. The pragmatic next step is to push credit unions and local regulators to accept non-fiat collateral like gold, crypto, tokenized assets, or land shares. With strong standards for custody and auditing or transparency, this will create an alternative finance ecosystem that's lawful, durable, and substantially independent of Fed-driven credit cycles.

These systems bypass Wall Street and keep capital circulating locally. Even if they deal in fiat, they are a good place to start. As the Fed crashes, they can more quickly transition to better currencies.

The Role of Technology

Technology is a force multiplier. Modern technology made with open-source software, public blockchains, inexpensive cryptography, and peer-to-peer networking, give communities tools they never had before. They can create money-like instruments, enforce transparent rules, and coordinate economic activity without Wall Street middlemen. Open finance primitives like tokenized assets, programmable contracts, and decentralized exchanges, can make capital portable, auditable, and programmable at low cost. Encrypted communication and modern key-management let organizers coordinate securely. Those features accelerate everything we want from local finance: faster settlement, clearer provenance of hard assets, community governance, and programmable savings/credit products that keep value circulating locally.

Technology is powerful but not magical. Governments still control legal tender rules, licensing, and on-ramps. Exchanges, custodians, and large centralized services can be regulated or pressured. Servers can be seized and platforms delisted. Because of that, don't fetishize purely digital solutions. Design systems assuming partial failure of any one platform.

It's best to work with open-standards and prevent locking assets into a single corporate silo. Educate your community about basic cryptography, custody models, seed phrases and the best ways to store them, and the operational risks of tooling. Opaque "black-box" tech creates fragility, not resilience.

CBDCs are a wake-up call. The government promises convenience, but these are nothing but mechanisms for more control and surveillance. That's why the movement to reduce Fed influence must be technology-literate. Push for privacy-respecting systems whenever possible. Systems are best that offer strong auditability to members without exposing transactional details to external authorities.

The biggest hurdle in technology is trust. People must understand why dollars are dangerous and why alternatives matter. Education is part of building the network:
- Teach neighbors how to use crypto wallets.
- Run community workshops on barter and local credit.

Crash The Fed

- Normalize trade in alternative currencies before collapse.

When a crisis hits, people will fall back on what they know. Make sure they know freedom.

Part VI
The End Game

Every new beginning comes
from some other beginning's end.
— Seneca

Part IV
End Game

Signs of Imminent Collapse

Collapses don't happen in a vacuum. They leave tracks. Before Rome's denarius was worthless, coins were already being clipped. Before Weimar Germany collapsed, prices were already doubling monthly. Before 2008, housing prices and leverage ratios were already screaming danger.

The Fed's collapse will be the same. The trick is knowing which signals matter. If you wait until CNN says "panic," it's already too late.

Sign 1: Exploding Debt and Interest Costs

The U.S. national debt is already past $38 trillion. That's alarming enough. But the real red flag is interest payments. In 2024, interest on the debt topped $1 trillion a year — more than the defense budget.

Once interest consumes a government's ability to fund itself, collapse is inevitable. It's the same death spiral that destroyed empires for centuries.

Watch the numbers: when interest payments eat most of the federal budget, the endgame has begun.

Sign 2: Accelerated Money Printing

Every crisis of the last 20 years — dot-com crash, 9/11, 2008 financial crisis, COVID-19 — was met with the same response: trillions created overnight.

Watch the Fed's balance sheet. When "quantitative easing" goes from an emergency measure to permanent policy, the con is near its end. The machine can only print so much before confidence dies.

Sign 3: Inflation Out of Control

For decades, the Fed pretended inflation was "2%." Then in 2021–2022, it hit 8–9% officially — double digits in real terms.

Runaway inflation is not just a number. It's the signal of a broken promise. When people stop believing the Fed can control prices, the spiral accelerates into hyperinflation.

Signs to watch:
- Grocery and gas doubling in months.
- Shrinkflation — smaller packages for the same price.
- Workers demanding monthly instead of yearly raises.

When everyday life feels unstable, collapse is no longer theoretical.

Sign 4: Mass Dollar Repatriation

For decades, the world tolerated the dollar as the "reserve currency." Nations bought U.S. debt, priced oil in dollars, and kept their reserves in Treasuries.

Now, that's changing. BRICS nations are openly trading outside the dollar. Central banks are stockpiling gold. China and Russia are dumping Treasuries.

The red flag: when Saudi Arabia accepts non-dollar oil payments, the "petrodollar" is dead. That will trigger a flood of unwanted dollars back into America, causing sudden inflation.

Nations hold dollars primarily because they exported something to the U.S., or they exported to another country that exported to the U.S. 60 years ago, when a country exported goods, they would stockpile currency from the countries they sold to. They could dump those dollars on a currency exchange to get back their own, but there wasn't always enough of their own currency available. This could crash the price of the currency they wanted to get rid of. That's not a smart plan if they want to get as much as they can out of that. Instead, they would send that money back to the country that issued it in exchange for gold.

This practice was famously stopped by Nixon in 1971, but countries can still buy gold, crypto, or land, in the country that issued the currency they are holding. That means that countries that hold a lot of U.S. currency and want to get rid of it fast will use it to buy anything of durable value like precious metals and cryptocurrencies. They might buy land too, but this creates more problems since they can't take it home with them. They can also buy politicians.

The end result is that you will see quickly rising prices in metals and cryptocurrencies. While this might happen from the dumping of a single currency, it can affect worldwide markets.

Sign 5: Bank Instability and Bail-Ins

Banks are fragile because they lend out most deposits. In stress, they fail fast. The government makes all kinds of assurances about protecting the financial system by printing an unlimited supply of money. Because of this, I don't expect banks to fail in the traditional way. There will not be a shortage of cash.

In many of the previous banking collapses of the last century, banks actually failed. There was a shortage of cash at the ATM, and banks were considered insolvent, having all their assets and accounts handed over to larger banks. That won't happen this time.

This time, the government has many other far more pressing issues. They have already lowered their reserve rate for the banks to 0%, meaning they can't be called insolvent. If they need cash, the government will print it, as they are less concerned with stopping inflation now than they have been in the past. Instead, they are more concerned with propping up confidence in their fake monetary scheme.

When the banks collapse, you will likely have full access to all of your accounts and cash, just like the people of Zimbabwe, Venezuela, and Germany. You may have so much access to your cash, that you can pick it up out of the gutter in handfuls. But the banks will still be there.

Keeping the banks open will only help to further accelerate the printing of money, so pay less attention to your bank, and pay more attention to the printing presses.

Sign 6: Gold, Silver, and Bitcoin Breaking Free

When people lose trust in fiat, they run to alternatives. Watch precious metals and crypto. If gold soars past $3,000, silver past $50, or Bitcoin beyond six figures while the dollar weakens, it means confidence is collapsing. (Between the time that last sentence was written and the publication of this book, silver has risen past $50, and gold past $4,300.)

These aren't just investments. They are barometers of trust. When they break free, it's the signal the world no longer believes in the Fed's paper.

It's hard to describe what is presently happening because it changes every week. By the time this book is published or by the time you read it, things may be very different.

Today, people are arguing over gold versus bitcoin. They think that something magical is happening and people are finally recognizing their value. Gold bulls claim crypto is collapsing because people finally realized gold is king. On the other side, crypto HODLers are calling gold a bubble.

Though both of these people are right to invest in metals or crypto, they are wrong to discount the other, and they are wrong about the markets. These assets aren't climbing in price because people realize their value. It's because they are getting rid of their dollars.

Photos are circulating on social media showing lines of people outside of banks, waiting to pick up gold or silver, but these lines are relatively small compared to the population. All of their purchases likely total some small amount compared to large investors who are buying large shipments, like governments that are buying metals by the ton.

Both metals and crypto are great assets. The world is not waking up to that. One asset is not proving to be better than the other. People are just trying to get rid of their paper funny money.

Sign 7: Political "Emergency Measures"

Every empire facing collapse grabs for control. Expect:
- **Price controls.** Outlawing "gouging" while shelves empty.
- **Capital controls.** Limits on moving money or converting it into gold/crypto.
- **Rationing.** Gas, food, medicine by decree.
- **Digital Dollar Pilot Programs.** The "solution" of Fed 2.0 rolled out as a rescue.

When you hear politicians say "temporary," remember: nothing is more permanent than a government's "temporary" solution to an emergency. They will offer emergency solutions to the problem they created. These solutions will grant them more power and control, and set us up for a new collapse just a few years later. All the while, we will experience less freedom and suffer a lower quality of life.

Sign 8: Public Panic

The final stage of collapse is psychology. Once ordinary people stop believing in the dollar, the game ends.
- Lines at gas stations.
- Empty grocery shelves within hours of restocking.
- A black market forming in real goods.

Confidence is fragile. Once it breaks, it never comes back.

Let the Signs Empower You

Each signal matters, but it's when they converge that collapse becomes imminent. You'll see soaring debt, hyperinflation, foreign rejection and repatriation of dollars, alternatives spiking, political "fixes" and public panic.

That convergence is the storm.

Most people will be caught off guard. They'll say "no one could have seen this coming." You will know better. You'll have seen the signs. That gives you an edge to convert your paper into value, stock supplies and strengthen community ties.

Crash The Fed

Collapse is only a disaster for the blind. For the watchful, it is the signal to act. The Fed's collapse will not arrive without warning. The signs are already here. They are flashing brighter by the year.

The empire of paper is cracking. The question is not *if* you'll see it, but *whether you'll be prepared and act when you do.*

Controlled Demolition

The Federal Reserve was never designed to serve the people. It was designed to control them. Every boom and bust, every bailout, every inflationary wave and "emergency" measure — all of it is part of a system that transfers power upward while leaving the rest of us fighting for scraps. The Fed is not broken. It's working exactly as intended.

We've spent this book tracing the machinery: how fiat money is created from debt, how inflation quietly robs savers, how taxation and regulation enforce obedience, and how global banking cartels coordinate to keep the illusion alive. It's a system of managed scarcity in an economy of abundance.

So let's be clear: **we are not here to reform the Fed**. You can't reform a counterfeit. You can only replace it. The mission is not a protest, but **a controlled demolition**. The Fed must be torn down piece by piece, while building the foundations of something real beneath it. We could wait for it to collapse under its own weight, but then the same people who built it will try to rebuild it again, with a new name and a digital leash. The only way out is to make it obsolete before it dies.

That means action. It means opting out wherever possible, and opting in to systems that serve people instead of parasites. Every chapter of this book pointed to a part of that blueprint.

We have to use and encourage the use of better currencies. Not just one. We don't need a law to say that everyone must use the same currency.

Crash The Fed

We need to create unity between the left and right. Everyone should be encouraged to take as much as they can from the government, and avoid as many taxes as possible. There are many legal ways to do this.

Once we get the money away from the government, we need to trade up for hard assets, and do whatever we can to keep them in our communities. Help to educate friends, family, and neighbors to do the same.

Technology will be a huge part of the system that takes down the Fed. Blockchain and encryption empower us to trade freely, but the same tools can enslave us through surveillance money like CBDCs if we don't understand how they work.

Don't put all your eggs in one basket. There are many valuable assets and you don't have to pick just one. Collect some precious metals, cryptocurrencies, and other valuable hard assets from land to ammunition.

Crashing the Fed isn't just an economic act — it's a moral one. It's the rejection of counterfeit authority and forced dependence. It's the reclamation of responsibility for our own value and production. The Fed's magic works only because we still worship its notes. The "full faith and credit," is a myth that stability requires masters. Once we stop believing, the spell breaks.

This is not a violent revolution. It's a **withdrawal of consent**. A refusal to play their game. A mass awakening where millions quietly shift their energy, labor, and savings into systems that cannot be inflated away. A peaceful, voluntary, unstoppable exodus from the empire of debt.

And when that exodus grows large enough, the old order will crumble. Not with a bang, but with the silence of irrelevance. The Fed will still exist on paper, but its power will vanish as people trade, save, and prosper outside its reach. That is the controlled demolition. That is how we win.

The beauty of it all is that we don't need permission, majority votes, or political miracles. We just need enough people willing to live differently — to build the alternatives, support each other, and refuse to be owned. The solution to tyranny isn't in Congress or Wall Street. It's in every community that plants food instead of buying debt, that mints honest currency instead of trusting counterfeit, that stands on voluntary exchange instead of coercion.

We don't crash the Fed by destroying what exists — we crash it by **making it irrelevant**. We let it starve while we feed what comes next.

Crash The Fed

This is how free people end empires:
Not through violence.
Not through begging.
But through creation, courage, and withdrawal of belief.

The Fed's walls are made of paper.

Let's light the match — not in anger, but in freedom — and build something honest in its place.

Made in the USA
Coppell, TX
31 December 2025

67862799R00089